→INTRODUCING
MARX

→INTRODUCING

MARX

RIUS

ICON

This edition published in the UK in 2012 by Icon Books Ltd, Omnibus Business Centre, 39–41 North Road, London N7 9DP email: info@iconbooks.com www.introducingbooks.com

Sold in the UK, Europe, and Asia by Faber & Faber Ltd, Bloomsbury House, 74–77 Great Russell Street, London WC1B 3DA or their agents

Distributed in South Africa by Jonathan Ball, Office B4, The District, 41 Sir Lowry Road, Woodstock 7925

Distributed in Australia and New Zealand by Allen & Unwin Pty Ltd, PO Box 8500, 83 Alexander Street, Crows Nest, NSW 2065

Distributed in Canada by Publishers Group Canada, 76 Stafford Street, Unit 300 Toronto, Ontario M6J 2S1

First published in 1994 as *Marx for Beginners* and in 1999 under the present title.

ISBN: 978-184831-407-8

Originating editor: Richard Appignanesi

Printed by Clays Ltd, St Ives plc

Editor's Introduction

This first English translation of Rius' *Marx para Principiantes* was originally published in 1976. It was an instant hit! I was his British editor at the time and I knew we were on to a winner when a local Tory party HQ in Kensington ordered a half-dozen copies. The popularity of *Marx for Beginners* clearly signalled the existence of a readership hungry for information on "big topics" which could be supplied by the revolutionary means of non-fiction comic books. This persuaded me to originate other *Beginners* on Einstein, Freud, Darwin and so on. This whole series has now been renamed *Introducing*...

In the early 1970s I was already aware of Rius as a legendary Mexican cartoonist, singlehandedly producing a weekly comic, *Los Agachados* (The Underdogs), for the delight and instruction of the underprivileged. Humorously, but with deadly accuracy, Rius enlightened his public on every sort of social and political issue. His wit got him into trouble with the authorities. Rius then had the genial idea of introducing Karl Marx to his readers. And so, the people of the barrios came to know this German heavyweight, "Carlito". The world was soon to follow and Rius' brilliant primer was to sell over a million copies in 12 languages. The huge international success of *Marx* tells us something interesting. It obviously meant that a basic primer on Marx was badly needed, not only among the poor of Mexico but in the supposedly more advanced and sophisticated countries too.

We are perhaps inclined to think of the 1970s as the fashionable "age of Marx". Karl might have appeared as a pop totem on T-shirts, though very few actually read him. Too difficult. But by 1976 the radical culture was not as optimistic as it might seem to us now. The heroic moment of the Vietnam protest, student movements and socialist hopes generally were over. Che Guevara had perished in his Bolivian misadventure in 1967, the social democratic experiment in Chile had been suppressed with almost genocidal fury by Pinochet in 1973, and the Portuguese revolution of April 1974 had withered away. Reaction had triumphed and the Cold War was coming to a conclusion, with definitive winners and losers. By the end of the next decade the Berlin Wall had disintegrated, and the Soviet command economy had vanished overnight without trace.

No one laments the passing of the Berlin Wall, except the apparatchiks and Cold War profiteers on both sides of it. What saddened me was the unthinking naive joy at the prospect of a neo-capitalist future, expressed by even those who ought to have known better. It was depressing to encounter lifelong "Marxists" in the streets who breathlessly exclaimed, "Isn't it wonderful what's happening in Eastern Europe?" What's so wonderful? To witness the unholy rush of Communist parties to change their names? The spectacle of self-professed Marxists suddenly transformed into born-again liberal capitalists? Was it really so hard to foresee, especially by those with practiced habits of Marxist analysis, that we were entering into a period of acute economic instability and nationalistic crisis in Eastern Europe which made civil war virtually inevitable? Are we shocked that the primitive accumulative phase of capitalism in the former Soviet Empire has taken the shape of Mafia-style criminality? What did we expect, that somehow Eastern Europeans would come to mature capitalism without going the same pirate route that we had earlier followed to arrive at transnational supermarket capitalism?

In the light of what has happened since 1989, it is high time for a reconsideration of what Marx was really about, warts and all, without dogmatism and sanctification. What was done in his name in the Soviet Union, in Eastern Europe, China and elsewhere, has for too long been passed off as "Marxism". The first thing to remember is that Marx was an economic critic and philosopher, not a prophet. He gave no blueprint whatsoever of "socialism" or"communism". What he has principally and essentially left us is a critical analysis of capitalism. "Marxism" is, and should be, nothing else but the means of criticism.

The closest to a programme proposed by Marx is found in the famous 10 Points of the *Communist Manifesto* which Rius reproduces in this book. Look closely at these aims, considered revolutionary when Marx stated them in 1848, and you will notice something curious. Although they have never been fully implemented, it is nevertheless startling to recognize how many of his aims have in part at least been adopted in many industrially advanced countries, not by revolutionary means but by parliamentary reform. The truth is, much of Marx's economic programme – nationalization, state education and so on – became the agenda of Keynesian state management in the 40s and 50s. Thatcherism and Reaganomics in the last decade have almost entirely succeeded in rolling back these basic social democratic reforms. We are being told, constantly, that we have no alternative to the capitalism shaped by the monetarist deregulated "free market". That is not the view Rius takes. He neither apologizes for nor disguises his confidence in Marx's ideas, and that's unusual these days. Rius has done his job by making Marx a little more familiar. The rest is up to us.

Richard Appignanesi
Icon Books

PREFACE...

WHAT?! TRY TO SUMMARIZE MARX? THAT'S NOT ONLY A
SACRILEGE (AS MOST "ACADEMIC" MARXISTS WILL SAY), BUT A
COMPLETE WASTE OF TIME — BECAUSE COMRADE KARL IS
SUPPOSED TO BE COMPLETELY BEYOND THE RANGE OF SIMPLE
MINDS.

MAYBE SO, MAYBE NOT. BUT I'VE WRITTEN THIS BOOK ANYWAY,
ON THE PRINCIPLE THAT THE WORST KIND OF BATTLE IS THE ONE
NOT CONFRONTED.

ANOTHER REASON FOR TRYING TO TAKE ON CHARLIE WAS MY
WISH TO UNDERSTAND HIM — AN AMBITION WHICH I HAVEN'T
SATISFIED.

MARX — LADIES AND GENTS — WAS TRULY A "TOUGH GUY",
A "TEUTONIC GENIUS" TOWERING OVER MUCH OF THE SCIENTIFIC
KNOWLEDGE OF HIS DAY. HE JUST WENT ON PRODUCING
PHILOSOPHY ON PHILOSOPHY, WITHOUT WORRYING HOW MANY PEOPLE
WOULD UNDERSTAND HIM. RESULT? A WHOLE SERIES OF HIGH-
LEVEL WORKS. REALLY HEAVY STUFF AND MUCH TOO DENSE
FOR THE ORDINARY READER. MARX IS HARD TO DIGEST!

THIS BOOK TRIES TO PROVIDE A "DIGEST" — AN EXTRACT OF
MARX'S IDEAS. SOMETHING EASIER TO GET DOWN. BEING AWARE
OF MY LIMITS (5TH. GRADE ELEMENTARY!), I AM HAPPY IF THE
THING ISN'T COMPLETELY INCOMPREHENSIBLE.

MARX HIMSELF HASN'T MADE MY JOB ANY EASIER BY FORGETTING
TO PROVIDE A SUMMARY OF HIS WORKS. I GOT EVEN LESS HELP
FROM ALL THOSE SCHOLARLY VOLUMES WHICH PRETEND TO
CLARIFY MARX, BUT END UP BEING MORE DIFFICULT THAN
CHARLIE HIMSELF.

AN ATTEMPT TO "POPULARIZE" MARX RAISES ANOTHER
PROBLEM — THE DIFFICULTY OF PUTTING INTO EVERYDAY
LANGUAGE THE PHILOSOPHIC AND ECONOMIC TERMS HE USES.
BECAUSE THERE AREN'T ONLY 20 OR 30, BUT 200 OR 300!
TO TRY TRANSLATING THIS NUMBER WITHOUT LOSING THEIR
MEANING IS REALLY DOG WORK. I HOPE THE AVERAGE
READER WHO GETS THROUGH THIS BOOK WILL HAVE THE COURAGE
TO CONFRONT THE COMPLETE WORKS OF MARX AND COME OUT OF
IT BETTER THAN I DID.

I SHOULD ALSO LIKE TO THANK THE ILLUSTRIOUS MARXIST THEORETICIANS WHO, WHEN I ASKED THEM FOR A HAND, REPLIED POLITELY THAT I MUST BE OUT OF MY MIND TO START SUCH A WORK. I REALLY APPRECIATE THEIR "SPIRIT OF CO-OPERATION" AND REGRET NOT HEEDING THEIR ADVICE BEFORE SETTLING DOWN WITH HERR DOKTOR KARL MARX.

AFTER THIS INTRODUCTION, IF YOU STILL WANT TO GO ON READING— BE WARNED! YOU DO SO AT YOUR OWN RISK. I CANNOT ANSWER FOR THE DAMAGES.

ONE LAST EXCUSE FOR THIS LIGHT-WEIGHT BOOK (BESIDE MY OWN IGNORANCE): THE STUBBORN AND INSISTENT PRESSURE OF MY PUBLISHER WHO LEFT ME HARDLY ANY TIME TO WRITE IT. I'M SORRY TO SEE MY EFFORTS HAVEN'T "JELLED" AS I WOULD HAVE LIKED.

IT'S INCREDIBLE THAT MARX, WORKING UNDER FAR WORSE CONDITIONS AND PRESSURES THAN MINE, COULD WRITE ALL THOSE _THOUSANDS_ OF PAGES WITHOUT EVER LOSING HIS WAY OR MAKING A BOTCH OF IT.

BUT THAT JUST GOES TO PROVE IN THE END THAT MARX IS MARX, AND RIUS IS ... WELL, JUST A POOR GUY!

LONDON IN
KARL MARX'S DAY...

CHARLES MARX ('KARL' AS HE'S CALLED IN GERMAN) WAS A JEWISH-GERMAN PHILOSOPHER WHO LIVED AND STRUGGLED FROM 1818 TO 1883. EVERYWHERE IN THE WORLD HE'S BLAMED FOR HAVING INVENTED

COMMUNISM....

Holy Jesus! The Anti-Christ!

BASED ON HIS WRITINGS AND IDEAS, ONE THIRD OF HUMANITY PRACTISES COMMUNISM, WHILE THE OTHER TWO THIRDS KEEP ARGUING ABOUT THEM...

MARXIST!

COPPER!

ANYWHERE YOU GO, WORDS LIKE BOLSHEVIK, MARXIST, SOCIALISM, LENINISM, RED, FIDELISTS, MAOIST, MATERIALIST, COMMUNIST AND SO ON RUB LOTS OF PEOPLE UP THE WRONG WAY...

Capital, class-struggle, labour-power, proletariat...

ACTUALLY, MARXISM TODAY DIVIDES THE WORLD INTO TWO CAMPS: THOSE WHO HATE HIM AND THOSE WHO PLACE ALL THEIR HOPES IN HIM...

and I'd mention a third group: those who don't know him...

MARX HAS SOMETHING TO SAY TO EVERYBODY: THERE'S NOT A MAJOR CHANGE IN THE LAST HUNDRED YEARS WHICH DOESN'T OWE SOMETHING TO COMRADE CHARLIE'S INFLUENCE...

Boy! He sure had lots of interests, the hairy old guy!

ECONOMY, LITERATURE, SPACE TRAVEL, THE ARTS, HISTORY, HUMAN RELATIONS, THE VATICAN, THE UNIONS, REVO- LUTIONS, SOCIAL CHANGES, EDUCATION, MEDICINE, INDUSTRY, AGRICULTURE, JOURNALISM... EVERYWHERE YOU'LL FIND A HAIR OR TWO OF CHARLIE'S!!

BECAUSE CHARLIE MARX IS JUST LIKE THE BIBLE OR THE KORAN: MANY QUOTE HIM, BUT VERY FEW KNOW HIM, AND EVEN FEWER UNDERSTAND HIM... (OR BETTER... MAKE HIM OUT...)

And he wasn't short of hair...!

KNOWLEDGE – AND PRACTICE – OF HIS IDEAS NOW MAKES POSSIBLE WHAT WAS IMPOSSIBLE FOR TWENTY CENTURIES: FREEDOM FROM THE EXPLOITATION OF MAN BY MAN...

IN SHORT:
IF IN EVERY SENSE WE'RE BETTER OFF TODAY, WE OWE THAT TO MARX ESPECIALLY...

That's not true!... I owe it to my Boss!

(SOCIAL SECURITY, PENSIONS, PAID HOLIDAYS, UNIONS, SCHOLARSHIPS, AND MANY OTHER VICTORIES ARE INDIRECTLY DUE TO MARX!)

ALL REVOLUTIONS, EVEN THOSE WHICH CLAIM TO BE SPONTANEOUS AND WITHOUT "PUTATIVE" FATHERS, HAVE A MARXIST ORIGIN...

Not to mention some constitutions...

You hear talk of that **** Marx even in the Vatican Council!!!

WORKER PRIESTS ARE ACCUSED OF BEING MARXISTS, SOUTH AMERICAN GENERALS TALK ABOUT HIM.
HE'S STUDIED IN JESUIT SCHOOLS.
OTHERS HAVE FLED CUBA WHEN IT DECLARED ITSELF THE FIRST MARXIST COUNTRY IN LATIN AMERICA...
BUT STILL YOU HEAR IT SAID THERE'S NO INTEREST IN MARX,...

WEST GERMANY (GFR)

EAST GERMANY (GDR)

BERLIN•

•BONN

•TRIER

HERE, IN THE
CITY OF
TREVIRORUM
(TODAY TRIER)
KARL MARX
WAS BORN,
5th MAY 1818

HIS FATHER WAS A WELL-TO-DO
LAWYER, WHICH ALLOWED
THE YOUNG MARX TO STUDY
WHAT WAS IN FASHION THEN:

LAW.

(Do what
Daddy tells
you to —
some fashion!)

What kind
of ideas did
they teach
then?

All kinds — but
we'll go into
details later...

BRIEFLY:
MARX WENT TO BONN UNIVERSITY TO STUDY LAW. BUT HE WORKED HARDER AT RAISING HELL AND (SO HIS TEACHERS SAY) PURSUING WINE, WOMEN AND SONG... TO SUCH A POINT THAT HE ENDED UP FIGHTING A DUEL FOR A LADY'S FAVOURS, WHICH EARNED HIM A WOUND ON THE EYEBROW! YOU CAN'T REALLY SAY THAT HE KEPT HIS NOSE TO THE GRINDSTONE...

Well, what do you expect of a 19-year-old?

FROM BONN HE WENT TO BERLIN WHERE HE FINISHED HIS STUDIES. THEN HE RETURNED TO BONN TO TRY TEACHING, BUT HIS BAD NAME DIDN'T OPEN ANY DOORS; IN BERLIN HE'D TURNED ATHEIST <u>AND</u> SUBVERSIVE...

What? <u>Both</u> at once?

THAT WAS TOO MUCH! HIS SOCIETY BARELY TOLERATED ARTISTS, SO JUST IMAGINE WHAT THEY MADE OF <u>SUBVERSIVES</u>.!!!

17

IT IS IMPORTANT AT THIS POINT TO CLEAR UP A DETAIL ABOUT MARX'S LIFE: ALTHOUGH HIS ORIGINS WERE JEWISH, HE DIDN'T CONSIDER HIMSELF JEWISH, OR EVER PRACTISE THAT RELIGION. HIS FATHER HAD BECOME A LUTHERAN AND MARX HIMSELF WAS ONE, BUT ONLY IN HIS YOUTH...

How true! Youngsters today don't believe a damn thing!

Blame the ideologies, your lordship, the ideologies...

THE UNIVERSITY OF BERLIN WAS IN A TERRIFIC TURMOIL OF NEW IDEAS. RELIGIOUS EXPLANATIONS OF MAN AND THE UNIVERSE HAD BEEN CHALLENGED AND THINKERS WERE LOOKING ROUND FOR OTHER ANSWERS TO THE ETERNAL QUESTIONS OF MANKIND...

Who is God?

Life is a Riddle

What is Man?

Why do we live?

What is Life?

The same old eternal questions

18

What's to be done?

THE YOUNG MARX DIDN'T ASK HIMSELF "WHAT TO DO?" IN THE SENSE OF "HOW CAN I EARN A LIVING?" BUT "WHAT IS THE MEANING OF MY LIFE AND WHAT PURPOSE SHOULD IT SERVE...?"

TO ANSWER THIS THORNY QUESTION, MARX DECIDED TO STUDY PHILOSOPHY...

Is he crazy, mum??

HIS FATHER GROWS ANGRY WORRYING ABOUT HIS SON'S FUTURE...

SOMEONE CALLED FREDERICK HEGEL SEEMS TO HAVE FOUND THE ANSWERS TO THE BIG QUESTIONS.
GERMAN PHILOSOPHERS GRAVITATE ROUND HIM, SOME TO OPPOSE AND OTHERS TO SUPPORT HIS THEORIES...
MARX BEGINS STUDYING HEGEL'S IDEAS.
TOO BAD THE GREAT PHILOSOPHER HAD ALREADY DIED, ALAS!...

1770-1831

IMMANUEL KANT (HEGEL'S GREAT PREDECESSOR) ARGUED THAT YOU COULD _SUPPOSE_ GOD'S EXISTENCE, BUT NO SYSTEM COULD _PROVE_ IT. HEGEL INSTEAD SEEKS TO JUSTIFY THE **IDEA** OF GOD... HOW? HEGEL PROPOSES A SYSTEM OF _PANLOGISM_ (FROM THE GREEK _PAN_, ALL, AND _LOGOS_, REASON).

(Note: a little dictionary at the back of this book explains some of these terms)

KANT separates science from religion...

HEGEL wants to make religion into a kind of science...

REASON IS CONSTANTLY EVOLVING IN HISTORY TOWARDS AN ABSOLUTE GOAL.
"WORLD HISTORY IS THE PROGRESS IN THE CONSCIOUSNESS OF LIBERTY."
GOD EXISTS ONLY AS WORLD-SPIRIT, WHICH IS REAL BECAUSE RATIONAL
(AND VICE VERSA).

God is _restless_, according to Hegel!

"It is in the organisation of the State that the divine enters into the real."

MAYBE THIS JUSTIFIES HEGEL'S GOD. BUT IT DOESN'T JUSTIFY ANY PARTICULAR _ESTABLISHED_ RELIGION OR STATE...

Am I making myself clear? No?

marx's student friend Köppen (by Engels)

WELL, HEINRICH <u>HEINE</u>, A POET AND DISCIPLE OF HEGEL'S, EXPLAINS IT MORE CLEARLY:

"Thanks to Hegel I learned that the 'good' God doesn't dwell in Heaven, as my Grandma believed, but instead that I myself, here on earth, might be God'..."

OR — GOD DIDN'T CREATE MAN, BUT THE OTHER WAY ROUND...

BESIDES WHICH, HEGEL DIDN'T BELIEVE IN THE IMMORTALITY OF THE SOUL. BUT PERSECUTED BY THE CHURCH AND STATE (IN THOSE DAYS ALLIED), HE WAS FORCED TO GIVE IN A BIT AND NOT ALLOW HIS IDEAS TO BE SPREAD AMONG THE PEOPLE. HIS IDEAS WERE — SO HE SAID — "NOTHING MORE THAN PHILOSOPHY" AND IT WAS NECESSARY THAT PEOPLE SHOULD STILL FOLLOW THEIR CUSTOMARY RELIGION...

Remember: He was a respected civil servant of the Prussian State...

BUT IT WAS REALLY HEGEL'S <u>PHILOSOPHY OF HISTORY</u> WHICH ATTRACTED MARX. ACCORDING TO HEGEL, HUMANITY ADVANCES AND PROGRESSES ONLY BECAUSE OF CONFLICTS, WARS, REVOLUTIONS; THAT IS, THROUGH THE STRUGGLE OF THE OPPRESSED AGAINST OPPRESSORS.
PEACE AND HARMONY — HE USED TO SAY — DON'T MAKE FOR PROGRESS...

HEGEL WASN'T TALKING ABOUT SOCIAL STRUGGLE, BUT ONLY ABOUT _RELIGIOUS_ STRUGGLE. HE WASN'T THINKING OF THE STRUGGLES BETWEEN WORKERS AND BOSSES, BETWEEN OPPRESSED PEOPLES AND OPPRESSIVE GOVERNMENTS... ONLY OF A PURELY "SPIRITUAL" CONFLICT, A STRUGGLE BETWEEN IDEAS...

WHEN HEGEL DIED, CONTRADICTIONS LIKE THESE DIVIDED HIS FOLLOWERS INTO "HEGELIANS OF THE RIGHT" AND "LEFT". THE LEFT DEFENDED THEIR TEACHER'S MOST PROGRESSIVE IDEAS, THE RIGHT STUCK TO HEGEL'S SPIRITUAL AND CONSERVATIVE SIDE...

That's when (1830) the terms 'left' and 'right' came into use...

LUDWIG FEUERBACH, A SUPPORTER OF THE HEGELIAN LEFT, WANTS TO PUT HEGEL'S THEORY INTO PRACTICE. HE DENIES THE "SACRED" ORIGIN OF ROYAL AUTHORITY. MARX IS 100% WITH HIM...

Looks like Feuerbach's a man after my own heart...

THE PUPIL RAPIDLY SURPASSES THE TEACHER: MARX IS MORE RADICAL, MORE CLEAR-HEADED AND MORE PRACTICAL THAN THE HEGELIAN LEFTISTS. MARX IS THE ACTIVE TYPE AND NOT ONE FOR BLAH BLAH BLAH BLAH BLAH

THE HEGELIANS GOT LOST IN ENDLESS PHILOSOPHICAL AND THEOLOGICAL DEBATES: THEIR MEETINGS ALWAYS FINISHED WITH MORE SMOKE THAN FIRE... TO AVOID ENDING UP NEUROTIC, MARX ACCEPTED A JOB ON THE "RHENISH GAZETTE"... THAT WAS IN 1842

MARX MADE SUCH AN IMPACT ON THE EDITORIAL COMMITTEE THAT HE WAS SOON MADE EDITOR-IN-CHIEF. UNDER HIS DIRECTION THE NEWSPAPER GAINED REAL PRESTIGE... SO MUCH SO THAT THE GOVERNMENT DECIDED TO SHUT IT DOWN...

Liberty is fine, so long as it's not used to show me up as a crook (even if I *am* one)...

POLITICAL JOURNALISM CAME TO LIFE WITH MARX: THE USE OF THE PRESS TO SPREAD IDEAS, TO CRITICISE BAD GOVERNMENT AND TO LET PUBLIC OPINION IN ON THE AWFUL MISERY OF THE PEOPLE...

A philosopher and honest journalist? Does he plan to die of hunger?

MARX WAS TRYING TO PUT INTO PRACTICE (AND INTO THE HEADS OF HUMBLE FOLK) THE IDEAS WHICH CAFÉ PHILOSOPHERS ONLY TALKED ABOUT.

MARX INVENTED DOCUMENTARY REPORTING WITH HIS ARTICLES ON THE PEASANTS OF THE MOSELLE DISTRICT...

YES, EVEN CHARLIE HAD
FEELINGS...
AT THE TENDER AGE OF 18
HE WAS COURTING A CHILDHOOD
FRIEND, JENNY VON WESTPHALEN.
SHE WAS BEAUTIFUL, RICH
AND CAME FROM AN
ARISTOCRATIC PRUSSIAN
FAMILY. (HER ELDER
BROTHER WAS MINISTER
OF THE INTERIOR
DURING THE VERY
REACTIONARY PERIOD,
1850-58.) HER FATHER,
A STATE COUNCILLOR,
HAD ENCOURAGED THE
YOUNG MARX TO READ
THE GREEK POETS AND
SHAKESPEARE...

MARX HAD NO MONEY OR WORK.
HOW WAS HE GOING TO SUPPORT
HIS CHARMING JENNY?
HER FATHER IS SERIOUSLY
WORRIED ABOUT HER FUTURE...

IN 1843, MARX TOOK HIS JENNY TO PARIS. HE ACCEPTED A JOB AS
CO-EDITOR OF A RADICAL MAGAZINE WITH ARNOLD RUGE ('LEFT'HEGELIAN,
IMPRISONED 1825-30, BISMARCKIAN AFTER 1866.)

... MARRIED 12 JUNE 1843...

Let's see if it's true that
two can live as cheaply
as one...

IN PARIS, MARX WORKED
ON ALL THE ISSUES
PUBLISHED BY THE
MAGAZINE
"FRANCO-GERMAN ANNALS"...

There was one issue...

WORSE, THIS MAGAZINE WHICH
WAS MEANT FOR UNDERGROUND
DISTRIBUTION IN GERMANY CAUSED
HIM LOTS OF PROBLEMS... BESIDES,
HE DIDN'T GET ALONG WITH THE
DIRECTOR, RUGE, WHOSE VIEWS MARX
DIDN'T SHARE, AND WHO CALLED
MARX "REALLY MULE-HEADED"...

WHY?
BECAUSE IN PARIS, MARX
HAD GROWN EVEN MORE
RADICAL AS A DIRECT RESULT
OF HIS CONTACT WITH FRENCH
IDEAS (BLANC-PROUDHON-
LEROUX) AND THE RUSSIAN
ANARCHISTS BOTKIN AND
BAKUNIN...
(AND MEANWHILE HE
STARTED STUDYING THE
ECONOMIC THEORIES OF
THE ENGLISHMEN,
ADAM SMITH AND
DAVID RICARDO)...

PROUDHON
FRENCH
PHILOSOPHER

HEAVENS!
even a German will
go crazy reading all
these books!

MARX'S FRIENDSHIP WITH ANOTHER
FELLOW-GERMAN, FREDERICK ENGELS,
HAD THE GREATEST EFFECT ON HIM.

THEY MET IN THE "ANNALS" HEYDAY, 1844...

(1820-1895)

THE SON OF A RICH TEXTILE MANUFACTURER, HE LEFT PRUSSIA IN 1842
TO WORK AS A BUSINESS AGENT FOR HIS FATHER'S BRANCH OFFICE IN
MANCHESTER. ENGELS WAS A RESTLESS 'LEFT' HEGELIAN ANYWAY, BUT FIRST-
HAND CONTACT WITH WORKING CLASS MISERY AFFECTED HIM DEEPLY.

MANY ARTISTS OF THE TIME HAVE LEFT US EVIDENCE OF THE TERRIBLE EXPLOITATION SUFFERED BY ENGLISH WORKERS...

BECAUSE OF THEIR SMALL SIZE (AND LITTLENESS OF THEIR WAGES) CHILDREN WERE EXPLOITED IN MINES AND OTHER KINDS OF INDUSTRY BY INHUMAN BOSSES...

The Swine!!

ENGELS WROTE "THE CONDITION OF THE WORKING CLASSES IN ENGLAND", 1845.
MARX HAD BEEN POWERFULLY STRUCK BY AN ARTICLE ON ECONOMICS WHICH
ENGELS WROTE FOR THE "ANNALS".
THEY BECAME CLOSE FRIENDS AND DECIDED TO WORK TOGETHER...

A truly historical meeting!!

MARX WAS SO UNPOPULAR
WITH THE PRUSSIAN
GOVERNMENT THAT IT
PRESSURED FRANCE TO
EXPEL HIM (1845).
HE MOVED TO BRUSSELS,
BUT WAS EXPELLED AGAIN.
DURING THE 1848
REVOLUTION, HE RETURNS
TO GERMANY AND
SETS UP THE
"NEW RHENISH
GAZETTE" WITH
ENGELS (WHO
FIGHTS IN THREE
BATTLES!).
MARX IS ACCUSED
OF INCITEMENT
TO ARMED
REBELLION, BUT
AQUITTED BY A
COLOGNE JURY...

Age? 30
Financial situation? Desperate
Work? Not one that pays...

MAY, 1849, MARX
IS EXPELLED AS A
"STATELESS" PERSON.
AND SO, AS A MAN
WITHOUT A COUNTRY—
A "CITIZEN OF THE
WORLD"- MARX BEGINS
HIS EXILE IN LONDON...

BEFORE SEEKING REFUGE IN LONDON, MARX AND ENGELS HAD TAKEN PART IN A SECRET SOCIETY CALLED THE "COMMUNIST LEAGUE" WHICH COMMISSIONED THEM TO PREPARE THE NOW FAMOUS

(Rest assured that we didn't earn a penny from it...)

COMMUNIST MANIFESTO

What a catastrophe children!

"A spectre is haunting Europe – the spectre of Communism. All the powers of old Europe have entered into a holy alliance to exorcise the spectre: Pope and Czar, Metternich and Guizot, French Radicals and German police-spies. Where is the party in opposition that has not been decried as communistic by its opponents in power? Where the Opposition that has not hurled back the branding reproach..."

AT FIRST IT DIDN'T CAUSE ANY GREAT SENSATION. BUT LATER, BIT BY BIT, IT BEGAN TO CREATE REAL WORLD-WIDE ANXIETY. THE MANIFESTO'S PUBLICATION TURNS OUT TO BE ONE OF THE MORE IMPORTANT EVENTS IN HUMAN HISTORY...

(so it begins: but more of that later...)

MARX REMAINED IN LONDON FOR THE REST OF HIS LIFE, IN THE DIREST POVERTY (THREE OF HIS CHILDREN DIED THROUGH THE LACK OF MEDICINES), CONTINUING TO WRITE REVOLUTIONARY BOOKS AND ARTICLES FOR THE NEWSPAPERS WHICH WOULD ACCEPT THEM...

Among others, the New York "Daily Tribune"...

ENGELS HELPED OUT AND OFTEN HAD TO SUPPORT HIM. THE LITTLE INHERITANCE MARX RECEIVED WHEN HIS FATHER-IN-LAW DIED WENT TO PAY OFF HIS DEBTS. A JOB IN A RAILWAY OFFICE HE WAS ABOUT TO GET WAS REFUSED HIM BECAUSE OF HIS TERRIBLE HANDWRITING...

(Judge for yourself..!)

MARX NEVER HAD A STEADY INCOME OR A PERMANENT JOB OR A BANK ACCOUNT... BUT WHAT HE COULDN'T EARN FOR HIS OWN FAMILY, HE WON FOR MILLIONS OF OTHERS THROUGH HIS WRITINGS...

DON'T IMAGINE THAT CHARLIE'S IDEAS WERE GREETED WITH WILD ENTHUSIASM BY THE PUBLIC. ON THE CONTRARY — NO ONE KNEW ANYTHING ABOUT MARX OUTSIDE A SMALL CIRCLE OF GERMAN EXILES AND A FEW INTELLECTUALS...

Marx's economic theories made no immediate impact on the debate inside the workers' movement or on other thinkers, except after his death (1883). This is true of his theories on value and surplus value, accumulation, exploitation, pauperization, crisis and appropriation, class struggle and revolution. But by the end of the century, several such theories were being hotly discussed within the workers' movement; while others were gradually accepted as absolutely valid.

THE NUMBERS OF HIS BOOKS AND REVIEW ARTICLES PRINTED WERE VERY SMALL. COMRADE MARX'S STYLE WASN'T TERRIBLY CLEAR, AND SO, VERY FEW WERE ABLE TO GRASP HIS DARING AND COMPLEX IDEAS.

IN FACT, IT WAS ONLY IN 1917, WITH LENIN'S VICTORY IN RUSSIA, THAT THE WORKS OF MARX WERE HEARD OF THROUGHOUT THE WORLD, AND STUDIED AND DISCUSSED...

(and put into practice by millions of people...)

Working in misery was not easy, and the Marx family of six became ever more proletarian in character during those London years. Sometimes Marx could not go out because his clothes were at the pawnbroker's. Even paper to write on was lacking, as well as the necessities for his family. During this Dean Street period, 1851, a daughter, Francesca, was born only to die in a year.

Jenny Marx describes the hard times in a letter to a friend: "Our three children lay down by us and we all wept for the little angel whose livid, lifeless body was in the next room. Our beloved child's death occurred at the time of the hardest privation, our German friends being unable to help us just then. . . Anguish in my heart, I hurried to a French emigrant who lived not far away and used to come to see us, and begged him to help us in our terrible necessity. He immediately gave me two pounds with the most friendly sympathy. That money was used to pay for a coffin in which my child now rests in peace. She had no cradle when she came into the world and for a long time was refused a last resting place. . ."

THE LAST 25 YEARS OF MARX'S LIFE WERE SPENT WORKING ON HIS MAJOR WORK:

WHICH HE DIDN'T MANAGE TO FINISH.

ONLY THE FIRST OF THE THREE VOLUMES HE HAD PLANNED WAS ENTIRELY COMPLETED BY HIM. THE OTHER TWO WERE PUT INTO ORDER AND FINISHED, ACCORDING TO MARX'S NOTES, BY ENGELS.

MARX'S LAST YEARS WERE FILLED WITH ILLNESS AND INFIRMITIES...

Das Kapital.

Kritik der politischen Oekonomie.

Von

Karl Marx.

Erster Band.

Buch I: Der Produktionsprocess des Kapitals.

Das Recht der Uebersetzung wird vorbehalten.

Hamburg

Verlag von Otto Meissner.

1867.

New-York: L. W. Schmidt, 24 Barclay-Street.

...migraines, depressions, insomnia, haemorrhoids, boils, nervous debility, pleurisy and bronchitis, pulmonary abscess — enough to kill anyone...

... AND IT DID...
MARCH 14th, 1883, MARX DIED AT HIS DESK.

HE WAS 65 YEARS OLD...

33

BESIDES THE HUNDREDS OF ARTICLES HE WROTE
FOR THE GERMAN, ENGLISH, FRENCH AND AMERICAN
PRESS, MARX PRODUCED THE FOLLOWING GEMS:

1841: ON THE DIFFERENCE BETWEEN THE NATURAL
PHILOSOPHY OF DEMOCRITUS AND EPICURUS

1844:
- ON THE JEWISH QUESTION
- THE CRITIQUE OF HEGEL'S PHILOSOPHY OF RIGHT
- ECONOMIC AND PHILOSOPHIC MANUSCRIPTS

1845: THE HOLY FAMILY

1846: THE GERMAN IDEOLOGY

1847: THE POVERTY OF PHILOSOPHY

1848: THE COMMUNIST MANIFESTO

1850: CLASS STRUGGLES IN FRANCE

1852: THE 18th. BRUMAIRE OF LOUIS BONAPARTE

1853: REVELATIONS ON THE COMMUNIST TRIAL AT COLOGNE

1859: A CONTRIBUTION TO THE CRITIQUE OF
POLITICAL ECONOMY

1865: WAGES, PRICE, PROFIT

1871: THE CIVIL WAR IN FRANCE

1867:
1885: } CAPITAL VOLUMES I, II & III
1894:

MARX'S WORKS ARE
CONSIDERED THE WORKING
CLASS BIBLE. YET IT'S ODD
HOW VERY FEW WORKERS
UNDERSTAND WHAT HE'S
WRITTEN. MOST OF
WHAT HE WROTE IS
ABSTRACT, AS DIFFICULT
AS MATHEMATICS,
BUT IT DID CHANGE
THE WORLD...

The Russian Revolution: the work of MARX

The Chinese Revolution: the work of MARX

EVERY SOCIAL
MOVEMENT OVER
THE LAST 100 YEARS
HAS BEEN INFLUENCED
BY MARX (CUBA,
CHILE, MEXICO,
VIETNAM, KOREA,
CYPRUS, HUNGARY,
CZECHOSLOVAKIA,
INDONESIA, POLAND,
TIBET, BOLIVIA,
GUATEMALA, CONGO,
ALBANIA, GREECE,
ANGOLA, EAST
GERMANY, ETC, ETC.

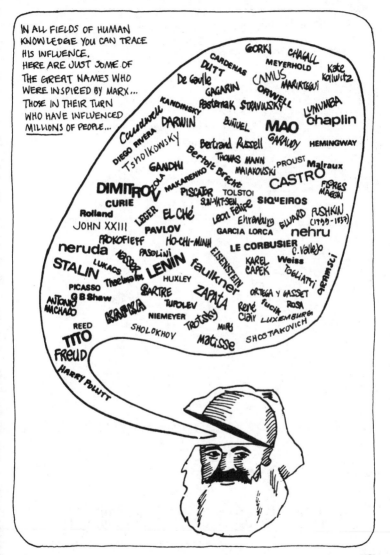

IN ALL FIELDS OF HUMAN
KNOWLEDGE YOU CAN TRACE
HIS INFLUENCE.
HERE ARE JUST SOME OF
THE GREAT NAMES WHO
WERE INSPIRED BY MARX...
THOSE IN THEIR TURN
WHO HAVE INFLUENCED
MILLIONS OF PEOPLE...

35

SO, AFTER THIS SHORT BIOGRAPHY OF THE MAN, LET'S GO ON TO SEE WHAT MARXISM IS, AND HOW CHARLES MARX ACTUALLY MANAGED TO CONTRIBUTE SO MUCH TO HUMANITY, LIKE IT OR NOT...

...WHAT HAS MAN BEEN THINKING THROUGH THE AGES?

IT'S NOT POSSIBLE TO GUESS WHAT MEN THINK IF THEY DON'T EXPRESS IT... EVEN LESS IF THEY LACKED THE MEANS TO WRITE DOWN WHAT WAS SAID...

WHAT DID THE FIRST HUMANS THINK?

.. Personally, I don't think that any of this is going to stay quiet...

IN THE BEGINNING, IGNORANCE AND FEAR PREDOMINATED. BECAUSE THEY DIDN'T KNOW THE MEANINGS OF THINGS, EARLY PEOPLES WERE AFRAID OF EVERYTHING WHICH MOVED, AND THEIR FIRST THOUGHT WAS ABOUT THE SUPERNATURAL: WHO MADE THE NOISE OF THUNDER? WHO MOVED THE EARTH? WHO MADE IT RAIN?

The Spirits!

THAT'S WHY, TO PROVIDE SOME KIND OF EXPLANATION FOR NATURAL EVENTS, MANKIND CREATED THE GODS: THE GOD OF RAIN, OF FIRE, OF EARTH, OF SUN, THE GODDESS OF FERTILITY, THE GOD OF HUNTING...

My god is more powerful than the dinosaur's...

37

OUT OF THIS CAME THE MAGICIANS AND SORCERERS WHO EXPLOITED THE "IDEA OF DIVINITY" FOR THEIR OWN BENEFIT. BY USING ALL KINDS OF CHEAP TRICKS THEY PASSED THEMSELVES OFF AS SPECIAL "DELEGATES" OF THE GODS WITH FANTASTIC POWERS...

EVEN SO, SOME BEGAN TO USE THEIR HEADS TO FIND LOGICAL EXPLANATIONS FOR THE PHENOMENA OF NATURE: THE "THINKERS"...

Stop thinking and find something useful to do!

Just a sec, I'm about to invent philosophy...

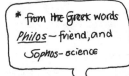

...to profit from it, of course...!!

PHILOSOPHY STARTED AS <u>CRITICISM</u> OF RELIGIOUS BELIEFS. BY SEEKING LOGICAL REASONS FOR THE THINGS IN NATURE, MANKIND CREATED THE <u>SCIENCE</u> OF PHILOSOPHY...*

* from the Greek words
<u>Philos</u> – friend, and
<u>Sophos</u> – science

THIS IS THE WAY GRADUALLY AN "UPPER" CLASS WAS FORMED- OR A <u>RULING CLASS</u>– AND A LOWER – OR <u>RULED</u> – CLASS... THOSE WHO LET THEMSELVES BE EXPLOITED AND THOSE WHO LEAD FOOLS BY THE NOSE (AND AVOID WORK...)

TWO OPPOSED CAMPS SPRANG UP WHICH STILL PERSIST TO THIS DAY:
RELIGION ON ONE SIDE, SCIENCE ON THE OTHER...

ONE OF THE VERY FIRST PHILOSOPHERS WE HEAR OF, A GREEK BY THE
NAME OF XENOPHANES OF COLOPHON, REFUSED
TO ADORE IDOLS, BECAUSE, AS HE SAID:

"If oxen and horses and lions
had hands or could draw with
these hands, horses would draw
pictures of gods like horses, and
oxen like oxen, lions like lions,
and the gods would resemble
the bodies each species
possesses..."

THE IDEAS OF XENOPHANES GOT ROUND, BUT
THE RULING CLASS WASN'T GOING TO TOLERATE RIDICULE OR DOUBT
ABOUT THE EXISTENCE OF THE GODS WHICH SUPPORTED THEIR
"SACRED AND LEGITIMATE" CLAIMS TO POWER...
BUT STILL MANY LISTENED TO HIM...

39

AS TIME WENT ON — AND PROFITS ROSE — THE RULING CLASS PERFECTED ITS RELIGION AND ADDED MORE GODS, MORE MYTHS, MORE RITES AND CEREMONIES. TEMPLES WERE BUILT IN WHICH GODS AND GODDESSES WERE WORSHIPPED, WHICH USUALLY MEANT "DONATIONS" OF MONEY OR OTHER THINGS HAD TO BE PAID UP "TO ATTRACT DIVINE FAVOURS"...

AT THE SAME TIME, A "DIVINE CASTE" SET ITSELF APART. WITCH DOCTORS HAD ELEVATED THEMSELVES TO THE PRIESTHOOD. THEIR POWER WAS SO GREAT THAT, TOGETHER WITH KINGS AND PHARAOHS, THEY CREATED HUGE EMPIRES OF FAITHFUL SLAVES "BY THE WILL OF THE SUPREME GODS"...

Show us some coin

The whole business went so far that kings too wanted to be worshipped as gods...

THE STATE COMMANDED WHICH GODS COULD BE WORSHIPPED OR NOT...

EVEN RELIGION HAD
TO INVENT SOME KIND
OF SCIENCE FOR ITSELF
(*THEOLOGY = THE PHILOSOPHY OF DIVINITY*)
TO JUSTIFY ITS EXISTENCE.

THE FIRST THING RELIGION
INVENTED WAS A FAITH IN
THE "BEYOND", THE
<u>AFTER LIFE</u>...

(The Egyptians were the first to fall for it...)

THE EGYPTIANS

THE EGYPTIAN ARGUMENT WAS QUITE SIMPLE: MEN WERE CREATED BY
OSIRIS AND MUST OBEY HIS WILL ON THIS EARTH.
THEY MUST PUT UP WITH SLAVERY IN THE HOPE THAT, IF THEY BEHAVE WELL,
A BETTER *AFTER*-LIFE AWAITS THEM IN THE NEXT WORLD — NO MORE
SLAVERY, ONLY ETERNAL BLISS...

GULP...

SOUNDS PRETTY FAMILIAR, DOESN'T IT?

HOWEVER, THE WORLD WASN'T TOTALLY DEPRIVED OF MEN (NO MATTER HOW FEW) ABLE TO RESIST BLIND FAITH, WHO PREFER TO COME TO THEIR OWN CONCLUSIONS, RELYING ON SCIENCE...

Who were they

Well ... Thales for instance...

THALES

OF MILETUS IS CONSIDERED THE FATHER OF PHILOSOPHY. HE LIVED FOUR CENTURIES BEFORE CHRIST AND DEVOTED HIMSELF TO ASTRONOMY AND SCIENTIFIC ENQUIRY INTO NATURE...

What is the force that keeps the universe in motion?

Pythagoras

ANOTHER FAMOUS PAIR OF WHISKERS — FATHER OF MATHEMATICS — CONCLUDED THAT <u>NUMBER</u> STANDS AT THE ORIGIN OF ALL THINGS, AND THEREFORE LIFE IS...

...The result of a perfect mathematical relation between the parts of a body...

PYTHAGORAS AND HIS FOLLOWERS (HE FOUNDED A PECULIAR SECT WHICH PROHIBITED THE EATING OF BEANS!!) WERE THE FIRST TO DECLARE THAT THE EARTH ISN'T AT THE CENTRE OF THE UNIVERSE...

Heretics! Atheists! REDS!!

AS A RESULT, THEY WERE PERSECUTED AND THE PYTHAGOREAN COMMUNITY WAS SCATTERED BY RELIGIOUS FANATICS...

NEXT CAME **HERACLITUS,** OFTEN NAMED THE FATHER OF <u>DIALECTICS</u>, THAT IS, THE ART OF ARGUMENT...

HERACLITUS, AN ATHEIST PHILOSOPHER, USED TO TEACH THAT EVERYTHING EXISTS AND AT THE SAME TIME DOESN'T EXIST... THAT ALL THINGS ARE IN MOTION AND FLUID CHANGE, CONTINUOUSLY APPEARING AND DISAPPEARING ...

"No one steps twice into the same river, for what occurs in the next instant is never the same as the first"

AH! YOU OLD FOX!

MORE OFTEN THAN NOT, THESE ENLIGHTENED FELLOWS WERE PERSECUTED AND ENDED UP BADLY. SCIENCE WAS FAR TOO BACKWARD AND IT WASN'T THE TIME TO TEST NEW "ATHEIST THEORIES"...

The structure of things depends on opposite tensions, as between the bow and arrow...

What kind of daft idea is that??

AND NOW WE'RE OFF TO SICILY...

AT AGRIGENTUM, EMPEDOCLES, ANOTHER PHILOSOPHER, USED TO CLAIM THAT HUMANS WERE ONCE UPON A TIME DESCENDED FROM GODS, BUT HAD BEEN CAST DOWN TO EARTH BECAUSE OF THEIR WICKEDNESS AND IMPURITY...

HE ALSO THOUGHT THAT EVERYTHING WAS MADE UP OF FIRE, AIR, EARTH AND WATER — A THEORY THAT SURVIVED RIGHT INTO THE MIDDLE AGES...

And which prepared the way for modern chemistry...

THESE FOUR ELEMENTS, SAID HE, WERE INFLUENCED BY TWO FORCES; ATTRACTION AND REPULSION, LOVE AND HATE, WHICH EXPLAINS HOW ALL THINGS IN THE UNIVERSE CHANGE ACCORDING TO THE RHYTHMS OF LIFE AND DEATH...

Love unites, hate divides. That's how change and motion happen...

HERE'S ONE MORE WHO DIED FOR HIS OPINIONS:

ANAXAGORAS...

AND YET HE SAID NO MORE THAN THE TRUTH: "the sun is a mass of fire and stone"... (AND NOT A GOD AS THE IGNORANT ATHENIANS BELIEVED)...

But the "worst" of the lot was Socrates!

Socrates

THIS GRANDADDY OF HUMOUR USED TO JOKE ABOUT EVERYTHING — ABOUT GODS, PHILOSOPHERS, GOVERNMENTS, RELIGION... AND ALSO ABOUT HIMSELF. AND IT'S TRUE HE WAS NO BEAUTY... SHORT, FAT, BALD WRINKLED, AND REALLY UNTIDY...

THIS WAS ONE OF HIS MOST ORIGINAL DISCOVERIES: HE DENIED MORALITY AS A SYNONYM FOR RELIGION... AND HERE'S HOW:

IN THE END, SOCRATES WAS ACCUSED OF CORRUPTING THE YOUTH, OF ATTACKING INSTITUTIONS, OF ATHEISM, LACK OF MORALS AND SO ON AND SO ON.

OF COURSE, THIS MEANT THE DEATH PENALTY, WHICH HE ACCEPTED BY DRINKING POISONOUS HEMLOCK FROM A BIG CUP.

BUT, IN BETWEEN SIPS, HE WENT ON TALKING CALMLY TO HIS DISCIPLES...

GREEK PHILOSOPHY ENDS WITH THESE THREE GIANTS:

PLATO, DEMOCRITUS & ARISTOTLE

PLATO USED THE <u>DIALOGUE</u> FORM TO EXPRESS HIS IDEAS.
IN THIS WAY HE POSED THE THREE MOST BASIC QUESTIONS OF PHILOSOPHY:

HOW CAN MAN DISCOVER THE TRUTH?

WHAT IS THE ORIGIN OF THE UNIVERSE?

WHAT IS THE PURPOSE OF HUMAN LIFE?

47

THE ANSWERS OLD PLATO GAVE TO THESE QUESTIONS LAID THE FOUNDATIONS OF A SYSTEM OF PHILOSOPHY CALLED "OBJECTIVE IDEALISM", ACCORDING TO WHICH ALL THINGS ARE THE MERE SHADOWS OF IDEAS. IDEAS ARE ETERNAL, WHILE THINGS ARE TRANSITORY...

Horses don't exist. What alone exists is the idea we have of horses...

TRUE KNOWLEDGE OF THINGS — SAYS PLATO — COMES NEITHER THROUGH PERCEPTION NOR REASON... OR, THAT IS, MAN CANNOT KNOW TRUTH BY MEANS OF SCIENCE BUT ONLY THROUGH "INSPIRATION" ARRIVING FROM THE BEYOND. MAN CANNOT KNOW THINGS ON HIS OWN, BUT ONLY BY THE IDEAS GOD GIVES HIM OF THINGS...

Platone

Needless to say... Plato wasn't executed...

HIS INTERPRETATIONS
OF REALITY WERE SURE
TO PLEASE THE
AUTHORITIES:
E.G. THAT HUMBLER
FOLK SHOULD SERVE
THOSE RICHER AND
NOBLER THAN THEY,
THAT THE POOR SHOULDN'T
WORRY ABOUT THEIR FATE
SINCE THEY WILL BE HAPPY
IN THE NEXT WORLD — THE ONE
TO COME, OF COURSE, NOT THIS ONE
WHICH IS JUST IMAGINARY ANYWAY...

A First for science goes to Mister Plato!!

LATER ON, IT'S WELL KNOWN, PLATO'S IDEAS WERE USED TO PROP
UP THE DOCTRINE OF THE "IMMORTALITY" OF THE SOUL AND THE
SINFUL NATURE OF THE FLESH — THAT IS, OF _MATTER_.

amen!

DEMOCRITUS

INSTEAD WAS PERSECUTED FOR
UPHOLDING "MATERIALIST" IDEAS...

"Cosmic substance is made up
of an infinite number of
elements or particles physically
invisible, indestructible and
infinite, which vary in size and
shape, and are in eternal motion"...

What's he talkin' about?

DEMOCRITUS WAS TALKING ABOUT

ATOMS

FOUR CENTURIES BEFORE CHRIST AND <u>TWENTY FOUR</u> BEFORE EINSTEIN!

THE GREEK EPOCH CLOSES WITH

ARISTOTLE

A REAL MASTER-MIND, A PROTÉGÉ OF ALEXANDER THE GREAT, A GENIUS IN ALL FIELDS OF HUMAN ENQUIRY (HE WROTE ON PHYSICS, METAPHYSICS, ETHICS, POLITICS, PHILOSOPHY, BIOLOGY, ZOOLOGY...) A REMARKABLE TEACHER AND A TIRELESS SCIENTIST. HIS INFLUENCE LASTED EVERWHERE UNTIL THE BIRTH OF MATERIALISM IN THE 18th. CENTURY

ONE OF ARISTOTLE'S MOST INTERESTING DISCOVERIES IS THAT SOCIAL CONFLICTS ARISE FROM THE INEQUALITY IN ECONOMIC AND SOCIAL CONDITIONS...

Some are rich and some are poor. AND the gods have nothing to do with **that**...

IT ALL DEPENDS—'ARY' THOUGHT— ON WHO'S GOT THE POWER. IF IT'S IN THE HANDS OF THE RICH, IT'S CALLED <u>OLIGARCHY</u>. WHEN THE PEOPLE HAVE IT, IT'S CALLED <u>DEMOCRACY</u>. THERE ARE MANY KINDS OF DEMOCRACY, WHICH AGAIN DEPENDS ON WHO PREDOMINATES— PEASANTS, ARTISANS AND SO ON...

SO, "ARY'S-THOUGHT-ALL" WAS THE FIRST TO REALISE THAT THE ECONOMIC SET-UP GIVES RISE TO SOCIAL INEQUALITIES. THOUGH IT'S ALSO TRUE THAT HE GAVE HIS O.K. TO SLAVERY BECAUSE IT WAS "NECESSARY" TO SOCIETY...

(Just as the slavery of women is justified because "NECESSARY" to the family...?)

51

ARISTOTLE FOUND PLATO'S
IDEAS RIDICULOUS.
HE CONSIDERED THE <u>SENSES</u>
AS THE ONLY SOURCES
OF TRUTH.

Seeing is believing...

HIS TEACHINGS ABOUT
ETHICS WAS THAT THE
GOAL OF
LIFE WAS
HAPPINESS.
SO, HE
ADMITTED THAT
ANYONE LUCKY
ENOUGH TO HAVE
<u>MONEY</u> OR
<u>POWER</u> OR
<u>HONOUR</u> WAS
BOUND TO
BE HAPPY...

(Those, first and foremost...)

THE FIRST PHILOSOPHICAL
ENQUIRY WHICH THE YOUNG
MARX STARTED ON, DEALS
PRECISELY WITH THESE
"GIANTS" OF GREEK
THOUGHT.
IT WAS THE SUBJECT
OF HIS Ph. D. THESIS
AT UNIVERSITY

"On the Difference
between the Natural
Philosophy of Democritus
and Epicurus..."

Phew!
It's hard!!

IF ANYONE CARES
TO READ IT, (IT CAN
BE FOUND IN SOME
LIBRARY NEARBY)
AND CAN DIGEST
IT IN A FORTNIGHT,
I'LL GUARANTEE
HE'LL BE A REAL
MASTER MIND...
(OR A COMPLETE NUT-
CASE IN A MONTH...)

PHILOSOPHY DOESN'T QUITE END HERE...
EVEN IF IT DID ALMOST VANISH WITH THE APPEARANCE
OF THE FALSE, BACKWARD CHRISTIANITY OF THE MIDDLE AGES...

(Knowledge becomes the slave of religious theology...)

NOT BY ACCIDENT, THIS UNBELIEVABLE EPOCH IS NAMED:

THE AGE OF FAITH

(AND BY 'FAITH' UNDERSTAND THE DENIAL OF _ALL_ SCIENTIFIC REASONING)

DURING THIS PERIOD, AT ROME, A FEROCIOUS DICTATOR-SHIP WAS SET UP WHICH DECLARED ANYONE A "HERETIC" WHO DIDN'T THINK LIKE THE CHURCH... EVERY TRACE OF PHILOSOPHY DISAPPEARS FROM EUROPE WHEN THE "HOLY INQUISITION" LIGHTS THE EXECUTION FIRES...

FRAR VBER TO

...And next, we will try to define the sex of angels...

DURING THESE DARK TIMES, SCIENCE AND THOUGHT DID NOT DEVELOP EXCEPT <u>OUTSIDE</u> EUROPE, IN THE MUSLIM WORLD, WHERE MEN LIKE AVERROËS AND AVICENNA REFUTED THE BIBLE AS FALSE, OR AT BEST AS "SYMBOLIC TALES MEANT FOR IGNORANT FOLK"...

△ An illustration of 'Erasmus of Rotterdam' censored by the Spanish Inquisitors because he was a "heretic"

IN THE ABSENCE OF PROPER PHILOSOPHY, A FEW, WHO HAD NOTHING BETTER TO DO, PASSED THEIR TIME IN THEOLOGICAL QUIBBLES ABOUT WHETHER ANGELS HAD NAVELS, OR THE IMMORTALITY OF LOBSTERS, OR THE MYSTERIES OF THE HOLY TRINITY AND THE CHURCH. THOMAS OF AQUINO WAS ONE SUCH WORTHY FELLOW WHO WROTE **21** VOLUMES OF MENTAL GYMNASTICS TO DEFEND THE DOCTRINES OF THE ROMAN CATHOLIC CHURCH...

(These are still studied today in Catholic seminaries...)

MACHIAVELLI (1469-1527) WAS THE FIRST TO COME ALONG AND ATTACK THE CHURCH AND PREACH REBELLION AGAINST THE DICTATORSHIP OF THE CLERGY...

The church has appropriated God for its own ends!

NOW BEGINS THE

RENAISSANCE

WHICH IS TO SAY - THE ALL-OUT COUNTER-ATTACK OF REASON AND SCIENCE AGAINST DOGMA, RELIGIOUS TYRANNY AND FANATICISM: AND IT SCORED AN IMPORTANT VICTORY FOR HUMANITY, THAT IS, FREEDOM OF THOUGHT...

I wonder why it is that the countries with the most nobles also have the most misery...?

BACON

THIS IS THE PERIOD IN HUMAN HISTORY WHEN FIRST-RATE MINDS SUDDENLY FLOWERED. PROOF OF THE VICTORY OF MIND OVER DARKNESS: DANTE, PETRARCH, DAVINCI, ERASMUS, LUTHER, VICO, COPERNICUS, GALILEO, KEPLER, NEWTON, BACON AND GIORDANO BRUNO...

Giordano Bruno (c.1548-1600), a Dominican monk and Galileo's contemporary, renounced obedience to his Order to follow the Pantheistic doctrine whereby God and Nature are considered as the active and passive elements of reality. Prisoner of the Inquisition, he refused to recant and was burned alive at the stake in 1600.

ALL OF THEM ARE GUIDED BY ONE IDEA: SEEK THE TRUTH INDEPENDENTLY OF THE CHURCH AND RELIGION.
BUT EACH ONE STAGGERED UNDER THE HEAVY YOKE IMPOSED BY THE CHURCH...

Reading through that list of renowned names, you perhaps wondered, 'Who the devil is VICO?'

"..Vico, Giambattista, a Neapolitan philosopher (1688-1744), author of the 'Principles of New Science Concerning the Common Nature of the Nations'..."

Mmmmm....

WELL, LET'S SEE:
THIS PHILOSOPHER FIRST PROPOSED THE IDEA (PRETTY BOLD FOR HIS TIME) THAT THE HISTORY OF MANKIND PASSES THROUGH 3 STAGES WHICH CORRESPOND TO THE 3 STAGES OF HUMAN LIFE:

INFANCY, ADOLESCENCE & ADULTHOOD... OR:

1 The state of barbarism and patriarchy of man the hunter, governed by magic...

2 The state of feudalism with a minority of lords and a majority of slaves...

3 The "New" state... the adulthood of humanity...

THE IDEA ISN'T ESPECIALLY REMARKABLE IN ITSELF, EXCEPT FOR TWO DETAILS: ONE, THAT VICO MAINTAINED IT DESPITE THE FEUDAL SOCIETY AROUND HIM, AND TWO, THAT HE SPOKE FOR THE FIRST TIME OF AN <u>EVOLUTION</u> OF SOCIETY TOWARDS DEMOCRACY THROUGH CLASS-STRUGGLE...

CERTAINLY, HIS MISTAKE WAS TO END HIS EVOLUTION HERE AND ASSUME THE BOURGEOIS STATE WOULDN'T BE CHANGED FOR THE BETTER, BUT ONLY THAT HISTORY WOULD START ALL OVER AGAIN FROM A FIRST PHASE ON A <u>NEW</u> CYCLE OF EVOLUTION...

DESCARTES & SPINOZA

With these two, mankind arrives at the use of Reason

WERE THE NEXT GREAT ADEPTS OF PHILOSOPHY IN THE XVII CENTURY, A TIME STILL DOMINATED BY THE CHURCH OF ROME...

POSSESSED OF A TRULY SCIENTIFIC SPIRIT, RENÉ DESCARTES WRESTLED HARD TO EXPLAIN THINGS FROM A MATERIALISTIC POINT OF VIEW, REASONING ABOUT THE NATURE OF THINGS, AND AT THE SAME TIME TRYING TO PROVE GOD'S EXISTENCE...

"All things we can conceive of clearly and distinctly, exist..."

THE CARTESIAN SYSTEM ("I THINK, THEREFORE I AM") WAS PART MATERIALIST, PART IDEALIST. HE BELIEVED THE HUMAN BEING WAS ONLY A MACHINE, BUT WITH A SOUL... AND HE EVEN LOCATED IT SPECIFICALLY: THE SOUL WAS HIDDEN IN THE PINEAL GLAND INSIDE THE BRAIN...

DESCARTES INTRODUCES US TO A MECHANISTIC CONCEPT OF THE WORLD. LATER WE'LL SEE WHAT THIS IS AND WHETHER IT'S EDIBLE...

SPINOZA LIVED A LONELY LIFE, FIRST BECAUSE HE WAS A JEW, AND SECOND BECAUSE HE STOPPED BEING ONE AND TURNED ATHEIST... SPINOZA PROCLAIMED SOMETHING COMPLETELY UNTHINKABLE IN THOSE DAYS:

> Man is free to think and believe as his reason tells him

GOD DOESN'T EXIST IN THE WAY RELIGION PREACHES, BUT—SPINOZA AFFIRMED—ONLY AS AN IMPERSONAL AND SPIRITUAL "PRINCIPLE", AS A SUBSTANCE WHICH CONSTITUTES THE BEAUTY OF THE UNIVERSE... (PANTHEISM BELIEVES EVERYTHING IS GOD). THAT'S WHY SPINOZA LIVED IN POVERTY, POLISHING EYE-GLASS LENSES FOR A LIVING...

BUT ALL THESE SEMI-ATHEIST, MATERIALIST PHILOSOPHERS HAD ONE FLAW: THEY PLACED TOO MUCH CONFIDENCE IN SCIENCE. THEY STARTED FROM THE ASSUMPTION THAT MAN IS PART OF NATURE (TRUE) AND THAT HUMAN RELATIONS ARE REGULATED BY THE SAME LAW WHICH APPLIES TO ALL OTHER NATURAL EVENTS (FALSE)

WHY IS THAT WRONG?

BECAUSE DESCARTES AND SPINOZA AND THEIR FOLLOWERS WERE WRONG TO BELIEVE THAT NATURE DOESN'T CHANGE, DOESN'T EVOLVE, AND THAT IT OBEYS ONLY ETERNAL AND UNCHANGING LAWS.

> Let's see how Diderot thought of it...

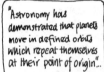

"Astronomy has demonstrated that planets move in defined orbits which repeat themselves at their point of origin"...

DIDEROT (AMONG OTHERS) CAME TO THE CONCLUSION THAT THE <u>UNIVERSE</u> AND <u>HUMANITY</u> HAD ALWAYS BEEN THE SAME. NEITHER HAD EVER UNDERGONE EVOLUTIONS, BUT BOTH WENT ON REPEATING THEMSELVES IN THE SAME <u>CYCLES</u> OF LIFE AND DEATH...

(These were – as we'll soon see – <u>metaphysical</u> and <u>mechanistic</u> concepts)...

Oh no! not more of that again!!

IN THEIR EYES, THE <u>PEOPLE</u> HAD NO EXISTENCE. ONLY "HEROES" EXISTED (KINGS, CAPTAINS, PROPHETS AND PHILOSOPHERS) WHO ACTED AS LEADERS. THESE WERE THE "DRIVING FORCE" OF HISTORY. CLEOPATRA'S NOSE – OR *HER BEHIND* – HAD MORE EFFECT ON HISTORY THAN ALL THE PEOPLE OF EGYPT PUT TOGETHER...

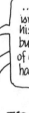

...and so if man isn't the master of his own destiny, but the plaything of a series of haphazard causes...

I'D LIKE TO...!

TO CONTINUE WITH THE PHILOSOPHY BEFORE MARX, WE RUN ACROSS THE

EMPiRiCiSM OF LOCKE, BERKELEY AND HUME

LOCKE (JOHN),

AN ENGLISHMAN WHO OPPOSED THE "DIVINE RIGHT" OF KINGS, THE INFALLIBILITY (ABSOLUTE TRUTH) OF RELIGION AND THE DOGMAS OF THE CHURCH... HE'S ALSO ANOTHER MATERIALIST-ATHEIST...

"...no man has the right to more than another because we are all equal, of the same species and condition, equal amongst ourselves, with equal right to enjoy the fruits of nature..."

LOCKE HAD THE IDEA THAT MEN WERE FREE TO THINK OF GOD IN THEIR OWN WAY, NOT AS ANY RELIGION TOLD THEM TO... THIS WAS A BIG BRICK ON THE HEADS OF PRIESTS, AND AN IDEALIST PHILOSOPHER, GEORGE BERKELEY, AN ANGLICAN BISHOP, TRIED TO REFUTE LOCKE'S THEORIES, BUT DIDN'T SUCCEED BECAUSE ANOTHER PHILOSOPHER CAME TO HIS DEFENCE...

DAVID HUME (1711 - 1776)

... AGNOSTIC PHILOSOPHER (BEING SOMEONE WHO DEFENDS THE IDEA THAT NOTHING IS CERTAIN). HUME SCANDALIZED ALL OF BRITAIN WITH HIS ANTI-RELIGIOUS IDEAS, AND SO HE HAD TO PACK UP FOR FRANCE, WHICH RECEIVED HIM A LOT MORE WARMLY...

61

FRANCE WAS A REAL HIVE OF THE MOST ADVANCED IDEAS. A WIDESPREAD REBELLION HAD BROKEN OUT AGAINST THE TYRANNY OF THE CLERGY AND THE MONARCHY WHICH FINALLY CULMINATED IN THE FRENCH REVOLUTION AND THE TRIUMPH OF **Reason** OVER RELIGION

Names!! C'mon! Out with 'em!

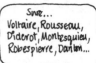

Sure...
Voltaire, Rousseau, Diderot, Montesquieu, Robespierre, Danton...

OF COURSE, THE FRENCH REVOLUTION DID MORE TO SPREAD POLITICAL IDEAS (SUCH AS LIBERTY, EQUALITY AND FRATERNITY) THAN PHILOSOPHICAL ONES. FOLLOWING ITS EXAMPLE, OTHER PARTS OF AMERICA FOUGHT TO FREE THEMSELVES FROM EUROPE... AND EUROPE FROM THE POPE...

These ideas liberated the world from the chains of religion...

(and with this liberation came the flowering of new sciences...)

AS THE EXACT OPPOSITE OF 17th CENTURY MATERIALIST PHILOSOPHY, AN IDEALIST VARIETY NOW AROSE, AND ITS GREAT CHAMPION WAS IMMANUEL

KANT

(GERMAN, 1724-1804)

Critif der reinen Vernunft

...

Immanuel Kant

Riga,

1781.

HIS MOST TALKED ABOUT WORK IS THE "CRITIQUE OF PURE REASON" WHICH COST HIM 15 YEARS OF CRITICAL ANALYSIS OF HUMAN THOUGHT. AMONG THE MANY OTHER COMPLEX POINTS BROUGHT UP IN HIS STUDY, KANT MAKES THESE:

"Every intent, whether scientific or religious, to define reality is nothing other than pure hypothesis..."

"Every attempt to apprehend transcendental knowledge is vain, since for every thesis the mind produces, one can oppose an equally valid anti-thesis..."

"It is impossible to prove the existence of God through any normal means..."

KANT WAS CERTAIN THAT THERE CANNOT BE MORALITY WITHOUT SOME BELIEF IN GOD OR IMMORTALITY, AND SO THIS OBLIGED ONE TO PRESUPPOSE THE EXISTENCE OF GOD AS A NECESSITY...

(IF WHAT WE'VE SAID SO FAR ISN'T CLEAR, DON'T WORRY. THIS HAPPENED IN THE DAYS OF "PURE" PHILOSOPHY WHICH NO ONE UNDERSTOOD OR TOOK ANY NOTICE OF EITHER...)

THE POINT OF OUR JOURNEY HAS BEEN TO ARRIVE HERE — AT <u>GERMAN IDEALIST PHILOSOPHY</u>, SINCE THIS WAS ALSO MARX'S STARTING POINT. SCHELLING, FICHTE AND HEGEL WERE ITS CHIEF EXPONENTS. BECAUSE OF THEM, PHILOSOPHY MAKES A GREAT LEAP FORWARD AND RECOVERS THE BEST OF GREEK PHILOSOPHY — THE <u>DIALECTIC</u> OR THE IDEA OF HUMAN DEVELOPMENT...

Metaphysics, dialectics, mechanistics, materialism, idealism... Hey! cut it out, will you!

Yeah! we're all going nuts!

RIGHT! MARX ALSO THOUGHT SO. PHILOSOPHY HAD BECOME A STRAIGHTJACKET OF JARGON AND MUDDLES, IMPOSSIBLE TO MAKE OUT HEADS OR TAILS. MARX SET HIMSELF THE JOB OF UNRAVELLING THIS CAT'S-CRADLE AND BEGIN MAKING PHILOSOPHY INTO AN EXACT SCIENCE, WITH LESS FUZZY SUPPOSITIONS, AND SO GIVE IT THE PRACTICAL MEANS TO **TRANSFORM** THE WORLD...

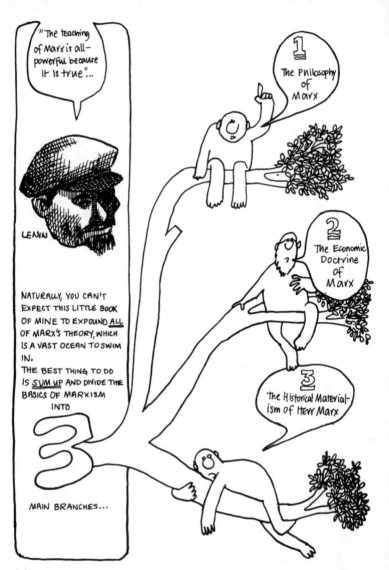

"The teaching of Marx is all-powerful because it is true"...

LENIN

NATURALLY, YOU CAN'T EXPECT THIS LITTLE BOOK OF MINE TO EXPOUND ALL OF MARX'S THEORY, WHICH IS A VAST OCEAN TO SWIM IN.
THE BEST THING TO DO IS SUM UP AND DIVIDE THE BASICS OF MARXISM INTO

3

MAIN BRANCHES...

1 The Philosophy of Marx

2 The Economic Doctrine of Marx

3 The Historical Materialism of Herr Marx

AS WE'VE ALREADY SEEN, THE PHILOSOPHICAL IDEAS OF MAN ARE OF TWO KINDS:

IDEALIST AND MATERIALIST

IDEALISM STARTS BY ASSUMING THE EXISTENCE OF SUPER-NATURAL AND DIVINE FORCES...

MATERIALISM CONSIDERS THAT THERE IS NOTHING BEYOND NATURAL THINGS...

IDEALISM IMAGINES THINGS, PRESUPPOSES THE EXISTENCE OF SPIRITS, "IDEALISES" EVERYTHING, BUT DOESN'T OFFER PROOFS FOR WHAT IT PROPOSES...

MATERIALISM, INSTEAD, DOESN'T IDEALISE, BUT SEEKS THE <u>SCIENTIFIC</u> EXPLANATIONS OF THINGS — INCLUDING EVEN RELIGION...

FAITH BY ITSELF IS ENOUGH TO GO ON

Or to put it more simply...

(... WHICH IS LIKE TRYING TO KNOW WHAT SUGAR TASTES LIKE WITHOUT SAMPLING IT...)

IDEALISTS EXPLAIN THINGS TO THEMSELVES THROUGH <u>RELIGION</u>...

MATERIALISTS EXPLAIN WHAT'S WHAT ON THE BASIS OF <u>SCIENCE</u>...

67

RIGHT AT THE START OF HIS PHILOSOPHICAL STUDIES, MARX JOINED FORCES WITH <u>MATERIALISM</u>. BUT HE DEVOTED HIS ENTIRE LIFE'S WORK TO GIVING IT MORE CONSISTENCY AND SCIENTIFIC CHARACTER...

Why?
Because before Marx, materialists were content to deny God's existence.
Period!
An' that's that...

"BY GOD'S GRACE", THE MAJORITY OF ATHEISTS WISHED TO PROVE THE NON-EXISTENCE OF GOD BY STARTING THE USUAL RELIGIOUS ARGUMENTS, WHICH GOT THEM INTO USELESS MUDDLES...

I'm telling you God exists!!

IN THE <u>XVII</u> AND <u>XVIII</u> CENTURIES, THE GREATEST SCIENTIFIC DISCOVERIES WERE MADE IN THE AREAS OF THE MATHEMATICS AND <u>MECHANICS</u> OF CELESTIAL BODIES. AND SO, MATERIALISM BECAME "MECHANISTIC"...
IN OTHER WORDS, THE MATERIALIST PHILOSOPHERS EXAMINED BOTH NATURE AND SOCIAL LIFE FROM A MECHANICAL POINT OF VIEW...

And that's why Diderot, Descartes and others are called "mechanists"...

DIDEROT

DESCARTES

BASING THEMSELVES ON MECHANICS, WHICH IN THOSE DAYS WAS THE HEIGHT OF SCIENCE, THE PHILOSOPHERS IMAGINED THAT THE SAME MECHANICAL LAWS COULD BE APPLIED AUTOMATICALLY TO LIFE AND TO NATURE...

Nature is immutable, subject to the cause and effect of rotary motion like machines... *

*THIS PHILOSOPHICAL CRITERION IS CALLED METAPHYSICAL

WHY METAPHYSICAL...?

METAPHYSICS, FROM THE GREEK, "PLACED BEYOND PHYSICS". *

IN METAPHYSICS, THINGS ARE UNCHANGING (I.E. IMMUTABLE), GIVEN ONCE, AND FOR ALL, WITHOUT INTER-RELATION SHIP, AND HENCE MAY BE EXAMINED INDEPENDENTLY, ONE FROM THE OTHER

HEGEL'S DISCIPLE, FEUERBACH REASONED LIKE THIS:

... nature augments only in quantity while always remaining the same...

(THOSE WHO THOUGHT LIKE THIS ABOUT NATURE, COULD THINK THE SAME WAY ABOUT SOCIETY TOO. SOCIETY CHANGES VERY LITTLE FOR THE METAPHYSICIAN, EXCEPT BY REPEATING ITSELF MECHANICALLY, E.G. WARS, HUNGER, GOVERNMENTS ETC...)

* ORIGINALLY, THOSE WORKS OF ARISTOTLE PLACED AFTER HIS "PHYSICS"

and mankind really can't do anything to change things?

69

HAVING RECOGNISED THE ERROR OF THE MATERIALISTS AND METAPHYSICIANS,
MARX ASKED HIMSELF THE SAME QUESTION:

AND MAN?
Ladies and Gentlemen...

LET'S LEAVE GOD OUT OF IT, AND ALL THOSE WHO WANT TO DRIVE THEMSELVES
CRAZY ASKING WHETHER HE EXISTS OR NOT— SO CHARLIE SAID—AND LET'S LOOK
AT MAN AND HIS ROLE IN THE WORLD. HOW IS IT REALLY POSSIBLE THAT NOTHING
CHANGES?...

INSTEAD OF THE
USUAL MECHANISTIC
NOTION OF NATURE
AND HUMANITY, MARX
AND ENGELS SET OUT
A THEORY OF
DEVELOPMENT—OR—
A RETURN TO

DIALECTICS

supposing it's edible...
how do you cook it?

DIALECTICS: from the Greek, "dialogue", to argue, to contend

WAY BACK IN ANCIENT TIMES, SOME PHILOSOPHERS HAD ALREADY APPLIED THIS STRATEGY TO ARRIVE AT THE TRUTH, A SYSTEM OF ARGUMENT WHICH BRINGS OUT THE <u>CONTRADICTIONS</u> IN YOUR OPPONENT'S REASONING...

RELIGION (CATHOLICISM ESPECIALLY) OPPOSED DIALECTICS BECAUSE IT DIDN'T PERMIT ARGUMENT. THINGS WERE JUST AS THE BIBLE SAID — AND <u>NO</u> DISCUSSION...

(...or else you discussed it with <u>me</u>!)

KANT AND HEGEL BEGAN TO RE-EMPLOY THE DIALECTIC METHOD.
BUT HEGEL NEVER BROUGHT IT DOWN TO EARTH; AS YOU CAN SEE FROM THIS:

" ... HIS HORIZON WAS FUNDAMENTALLY RESTRICTED BY THE KNOWLEDGE AND CONCEPTS CURRENT IN HIS DAY. ONE SHOULD ADD THAT HEGEL WAS AN IDEALIST, AND FOR HIM, THE IDEAS WERE NOT MORE OR LESS ABSTRACT IMAGES OF OBJECTS; ON THE CONTRARY, THINGS AND THEIR DEVELOPMENT WERE A PROJECTION OF IDEAS WHICH HAD EXISTED, NO ONE CAN SAY HOW, EVEN BEFORE THE WORLD ITSELF EXISTED. HEGEL'S SYSTEM WAS A GIGANTIC MISCARRIAGE, BUT THE LAST OF ITS KIND. WHILE ON ONE HAND IT AFFIRMS A FORMULA ESSENTIAL TO THE CONCEPT OF HISTORY, ACCORDING TO WHICH HUMAN HISTORY IS A PROCESS OF DEVELOPMENT WHICH CANNOT, GIVEN ITS NATURE...

Got it now?

You're joking

IN ESSENCE:

HEGEL'S PHILOSOPHY CONTAINS LOTS OF VALUABLE IDEAS, SUCH AS HIS THEORY OF ETERNAL MOTION, THE DEVELOPMENT OF UNIVERSAL SPIRIT, AND ESPECIALLY HIS METHOD OF

Dialectics

HE WAS RIGHT WHEN HE SAID THE LAW OF DIALECTICS GOVERNS THE DEVELOPMENT OF SPIRIT (MIND). BUT HE DIDN'T GO FAR ENOUGH AND APPLY IT TO NATURE AND SOCIETY..!

What's all this?

Well,... JUST LOOK

FROM THE STANDPOINT OF THE DIALECTICAL METHOD, NOTHING IS ETERNAL OR UNCHANGING... BUT IN SPITE OF THIS HEGEL DENIES THE DEVELOPMENT OF NATURE AND SOCIETY, THIS IS THE MOST SERIOUS CONTRADICTION IN HIS USE OF THE METHOD...

Now how's about an example even I can understand!

HEGEL (AND I'LL TRY HARD TO BE CLEAR) WAS AN IDEALIST. "THE ESSENCE OF REALITY," HE SAID, "ISN'T MATERIAL, BUT SPIRITUAL (OR MENTAL), AND IS THEREFORE INDEPENDENT AND THUS FREE..."

Great! Now explain *that*..!

Sure! Hegel says that you can feel free even in chains...

HEGEL'S ADVICE TO ANY WORKER EXPLOITED BY HIS BOSS WOULD BE: DON'T WORRY YOURSELF ABOUT MATERIAL OPPRESSION, BUT ONLY ABOUT THE "SPIRITUAL" KIND. BY OBEYING THE STATE (GOD'S REPRESENTATIVE ON EARTH) YOU WILL FIND HAPPINESS AND FREEDOM (OF THE SPIRIT...)

What the 'ell's he saying?

TODAY, HEGEL'S IDEAS SEEM ABSURD. BUT IN HIS DAY, THEY SOUNDED PRETTY DARING, AND THEY WERE ATTACKED JUST BECAUSE THEY WERE (IN THEIR OWN WAY) DIALECTICAL...

Dialectic... yes, but *idealist*...

THIS LED MARX TO SAY THAT HEGEL'S METHOD WAS "INVERTED", UPSIDE-DOWN, AND IT NEEDED TO BE STOOD ON ITS FEET AGAIN...

...in short, to make it Materialist...

But what does Hegel's theory say about Development?

Well, Let's take it step by step:

HUMAN DEVELOPMENT— SAID HEGEL— HAD GONE THROUGH CONSTANT EVOLUTION, STARTING WITH PRIMITIVE ORIENTAL DESPOTISM, IN WHICH ONLY ONE PERSON WAS FREE (THE TYRANT), AND NEXT THE GRAECO-ROMAN ARISTOCRATIC SYSTEM IN WHICH MANY MORE WERE FREE…

LATER STILL, SLAVERY AND SERFDOM DISAPPEARED, AND EVEN MORE PEOPLE WERE FREE… AFTER THE HOLY ROMAN-GERMAN EMPIRE, FEUDALISM, MONARCHY, THE FRENCH REVOLUTION, AND FINALLY WITH THE <u>PRUSSIAN STATE</u> HUMANITY REACHES (ACCORDING TO HEGEL, ANYWAY)

ABSOLUTE
<u>LIBERTY</u>

My, I <u>DO</u> like this chap Hegel. Give him the National Award.

PRUSSIA HAD AN EMPEROR, AN ARMY, A VERY RICH CHURCH AND SOME BIG LANDOWNERS. THE PEOPLE WORKED FOR THEM, WITHOUT BEING SLAVES MAYBE, BUT OPPRESSED ENOUGH. HEGEL DIDN'T NOTICE THIS OPPRESSION. HE IMAGINED ABSOLUTE LIBERTY EXISTED JUST BECAUSE SLAVERY WAS ABOLISHED…

WHAT WAS REALLY HAPPENING WAS THAT FEUDALISM HAD GRADUALLY GIVEN WAY TO CAPITALISM A MORE MODERN AND SUBTLER FORM OF EXPLOITATION.

... Doctor Hegel didn't take any notice of this...

But MARX did!!

HEGEL WENT ON TALKING ABOUT HUMAN DEVELOPMENT WHILE DENYING IT, BECAUSE HE CLAIMED THE PRUSSIAN STATE HAD BEGUN TO ACHIEVE THIS DEVELOPMENT ALREADY. SO HE TOO SINKS BACK INTO METAPHYSICS...

...Isn't that just like a Government Minister!!

HEGEL'S ARGUMENTS REMAIN VALID AND DIALECTICAL, EVEN THOUGH MISTAKENLY APPLIED BY HIM TO REALITY... LET'S SEE, FOR INSTANCE, WHAT HE MAKES OF THE "CONFLICT BETWEEN CONTRARIES"...

"Each thing is a combination of contraries because it is made up of elements which, although linked together, at the same time eliminate one another..."

DON'T HAVE A NERVOUS BREAKDOWN YET,! THERE'S AN EXAMPLE COMING:

SOCIETY, FOR EXAMPLE, IS A COMBINATION OF CONTRARIES (THE RICH AND WELL-OFF *VERSUS* THE POOR AND MISERABLE) HITCHED TOGETHER, YES, BUT OPPOSED...

If ya' wanna' stick with me, TOIL, man, TOIL!!

WITH VERY GOOD REASON, HEGEL SAID THAT WHAT MAKES HUMANITY EVOLVE IS THE STRUGGLE BETWEEN CONTRARIES.
THE TRIUMPH OF ONE OVER THE OTHER PRODUCES CHANGE...

But this dialectical law wasn't supposed to apply to REALITY...

FUNNY, HOW IN HEGEL'S PRUSSIAN STATE THE CONFLICT BETWEEN CONTRARIES WASN'T GOING TO LEAD TO TRANSFORMATION, BUT RATHER AN IMPROVEMENT OF SOCIETY.
THIS SUITED HEGEL, NATURALLY... THAT'S WHY!...

AT THIS POINT, MARX STEPS IN TO PUT HEGEL (AND HIS METHOD) THE RIGHT WAY UP...

HEGEL

... Between *real* contraries, such as capital and labour, no reconciliation is possible.

Is that clear..?

IF HEGEL'S DIALECTICAL METHOD INFLUENCED MARX, LUDWIG FEUERBACH (PRONOUNCED "FOY-ER-BACK") TURNED HIM INTO A MATERIALIST.

BUT MARX TOOK OVER FEUERBACH'S THEORY AND CHANGED IT...

What did this bloke Foy-er-back say and how did Marx change it?

FEUERBACH, A DISCIPLE OF THE IDEALIST HEGEL, GAVE UP HEGELIAN IDEALISM TO SWITCH OVER TO MATERIALISM, BUT OF A <u>METAPHYSICAL</u> BRAND, BECAUSE HE SAW NATURE (AND SOCIETY TOO) SUNK IN SLEEP, MOTIVE-AND-MOTIONLESS, WITH NO IMMEDIATE CHANCE FOR CHANGE

THAT IS:

Hegel was dialectical; but idealist... Feuerbach was materialist, but metaphysical (non-dialectical)

IT WAS UP TO MARX TO RE-SHUFFLE THE DECK: TO AMALGAMATE THE THE BEST OF THIS ONE AND THAT ONE AND COME UP WITH HIS OWN FAMOUS, UNIQUE VARIETY OF

DIALECTICAL MATERIALISM

(Dialectics by G.W.F. Hegel and Materialism by L. Feuerbach)

aargh! Marx made a merger

No! He improved, corrected and enriched them...

AS WE'VE NOTED, HEGEL DIDN'T SEE OR DIDN'T WISH TO SEE THE EXPLOITATION OF THE MAJORITY BY A MINORITY OF THE PRIVILEGED RICH. HERE'S THE FIRST QUESTION THE YOUNG MARX ASKED HIMSELF...

Work alienates the worker... But how and why?

(ALIENATION means 'to distract; to seize possession of something, to extort from others' what belongs to them'.)

UNFREE LABOUR, (IE. WHAT'S DONE FOR A BOSS) MAY EARN THE WORKER A WAGE, BUT AT THE SAME TIME IT "ALIENATES" HIM. IT DEPRIVES HIM OF SOMETHING WHICH GOES INTO THE BOSS'S POCKET.

But is this "something" money or what?

IN HIS FIRST WORK, MARX BEGINS TO INVESTIGATE ALIENATION — OR BETTER, THE DIFFERENT KINDS OF ALIENATION: POLITICAL, RELIGIOUS AND ECONOMIC

This work's called "Economic and Philosophic Manuscripts of 1844"

Marx wonders: where does the product of the workingman's labour end up?

BY HIS LABOUR, A WORKER MAKES SOMETHING (CLOTH, MACHINERY, TYRES, BOOKS, HOUSES...). BUT THIS OBJECT, BY THE FACT OF REMAINING THE BOSS'S PROPERTY, TURNS HEY PRESTO! INTO MERCHANDISE (A COMMODITY)...

LABOUR OBVIOUSLY DOESN'T PRODUCE THINGS FOR THE IMMEDIATE BENEFIT OF THE WORKER WHO MAKES THEM. RATHER, IT IS GRIST FOR SOMEONE ELSE'S MILL...

Alienation begins with the worker being squeezed dry...

"... THE ALIENATION OF THE WORKER IS EXPRESSED THUS: THE MORE HE PRODUCES, THE LESS HE CAN CONSUME; THE MORE VALUE HE CREATES, THE LESS VALUE HE HAS... LABOUR PRODUCES FABULOUS THINGS FOR THE RICH, BUT MISERY FOR THE POOR, MACHINES REPLACE LABOUR, AND JOBS DIMINISH, WHILE OTHER WORKERS TURN INTO MACHINES..."

(Marx: "Manuscripts of 1844")

(This is how alienation makes its victims...)

ALIENATION NOT ONLY DEGRADES MAN, BUT ALSO DE-PERSONALISES HIM. WHAT CAN YOU EXPECT?

MARX STATES: THE BOSS IMPOSES THE KIND OF WORK, THE METHOD AND THE RHYTHM, BUT HE NEVER BOTHERS IF THE WORKER ENDS UP AS:

A mere appendage of flesh on a machine of iron...

(Marx)

MARX GOES EVEN FURTHER AND AFFIRMS: THE COMBINED MEANS OF PRODUCTION NOW IN EXISTENCE HAVE BEEN PRODUCED BY THE LABOUR OF PREVIOUS GENERATIONS WHO HAVE THOUGHT, CREATED AND GIVEN THEIR LIVES TO ATTAIN SOMETHING...

So? Who owns the inventions of Galileo, Newton, Leonardo, and thousands of others?

NO ENTRY PRIVATE PROPERTY

IS IT RIGHT THAT ALL OF THIS SHOULD REMAIN IN THE HANDS OF THE FEW? THAT THE INVENTION AND LABOUR OF THOUSANDS OF YEARS SHOULD BE THE EXCLUSIVE PRIVILEGE OF THE WEALTHY FEW? NO, IT'S NOT RIGHT!

PRIVATE OWNERSHIP OF THE MEANS OF PRODUCTION IS THE MAXIMUM FORM OF ALIENATION...

"SOCIAL POTENTIAL HAS BECOME THE PRIVATE POWER OF THE FEW." MARX ALSO SUBMITS: THE LABOUR OF THE MANY TRANSFORMS ITSELF INTO THE CAPITAL OF A PRIVILEGED FEW.

THE ROOTS OF CAPITALISM

AND SO—MARX CONCLUDES—THE DEEPEST
ESSENCE OF MAN, HIS CREATIVE ACT, HAS BEEN
TRANSFORMED INTO A <u>POSSESSION</u>...

THE WORKER'S LABOUR
BECOMES MERCHANDISE IN
THE HANDS OF THE OWNER,
DEAD LABOUR, <u>POSSESSION</u>,
WEALTH, AND THE GREATER
THE CAPITALIST'S PROPERTY
BECOMES, THE MORE
IMPOVERISHED THE
WORKER'S <u>BEING</u>...

"The less you are, the more
you'll have. To have more,
you must alienate yourself."
You good-for-nothing!!!

Which changes
into a thing...

THAT BLESSED "LIBERTY" HEGEL TALKED ABOUT, JUST DOESN'T EXIST.
MONEY OBLIGES THOSE WHO HAVEN'T GOT ANY, TO SELL THEMSELVES
BODY AND SOUL — THAT IS, TO SELL THEIR LABOUR-POWER (WORKER,
PEASANT, INTELLECTUAL)... THIS IS ALIENATION:

EXPLOITATION...

TO POSSESS POSSESSIONS, A MAN WILL "SELL HIMSELF" TO HAVE WHAT ANOTHER HAS. BUT IT NEVER DAWNS ON HIM ~ THAT THE MORE HE GETS, THE LESS HE KEEPS OF HIMSELF...

This guy too aspires to own property. The purpose of his life is to possess more and more and more and...

Bye-bye homo sapiens...

THE COUNTLESS EVILS OF THE WORLD STEM FROM THE "DEFENCE" OF PRIVATE PROPERTY: THE EVILS OF ENVY, WAR, EGOISM, CRIME, INJUSTICE, THE MISERY OF THE MASSES AND LUXURY FOR THE VERY FEW...

I have a hunch that this fellow Marx is going to cause us many a headache...

HOW CAN THIS STATE OF AFFAIRS BE CHANGED?

In no way!! Who's going to tangle with the rich, the powerful, the church..?

MARX SINGLED OUT THE EXISTENCE OF A "NEW" CLASS:

The Proletariat

WHICH CAME TO LIFE WITH THE INDUSTRIAL REVOLUTION WHEN MACHINES BEGAN REPLACING THE CRAFTSMEN OF THE PAST...

a proletarian: someone at the beck and call of the boss's machines...

Marx predicted that this class— the working class— was going to change things...

HOW, AND WITH WHAT POWERS??

UNLIKE THE SMALL-SCALE ARTISANS WHO USED TO OWN THE TOOLS OF THEIR TRADE, THE PROLETARIAT OWNS NOTHING AT ALL— NEITHER THE MEANS, NOR THE END-PRODUCTS...

and still less our labour...

UNLIKE ALL OTHER SOCIAL CLASSES, THE WORKING CLASS POSSESSES ONLY ITS LABOUR POWER, I.E. WHAT IS COMMONLY KNOWN AS THE "WORK FORCE".

GULP!

DIALECTICALLY SPEAKING, THIS IS WHAT SPECIFIES THE STRUGGLE BETWEEN THE CONTRARIES: CAPITAL ON ONE SIDE, LABOUR ON THE OTHER. THEY LIVE TOGETHER, SURE, BUT WITH OPPOSED INTERESTS...

THE OUTLINES OF THE PROBLEM ARE CLEAR: IT ONLY REQUIRES PRACTICAL PROOF, NOT THE WAYWARD LANGUAGE OF PHILOSOPHY WHICH BAFFLES EVERYONE...

Private property has made us so stupid and one-sided that an object is only *ours* when we have it — when it exists for us as capital, or when it is directly possessed, eaten, drunk, worn, inhabited, etc.,—in short, when it is *used* by us . . .

In place of *all* these physical and mental senses there has therefore come the sheer alienation of *all* these senses — the sense of *having*. The human being had to be reduced to this absolute poverty in order that he might yield his inner wealth to the outer world . . .

In order to abolish the *idea* of private property, the *idea* of communism is completely sufficient. It takes *actual* communist action to abolish actual private property. History will come to it; and this movement, which in *theory* we already know to be a self-transcending movement, will constitute *in actual fact* a very severe and protracted process . . .

1844

Marx (extracts from *Manuscripts of 1844*)

Sorry!!

IN HIS "MANUSCRIPTS OF 1844", MARX STILL SPEAKS LIKE A PURE PHILOSOPHER, WITHOUT REAL CONTACT WITH THE WORKING CLASS WHICH HE IS ONLY DISCOVERING. HE WON'T REALLY SEE THINGS CLEARLY UNTIL HE FREES HIMSELF FROM BOURGEOIS CONCEPTIONS AND STARTS VIEWING REALITY FROM A PROLETARIAN ANGLE...

THE REASON'S QUITE SIMPLE: THE ONLY PHILOSOPHY AROUND WAS BOURGEOIS, NOT PROLETARIAN ... A PHILOSOPHY RESTRICTED TO THE FEW...

The working class doesn't have a philosophy of its own!

THAT'S WHAT MARX RECOGNIZED, AND SO HE SPENT HIS LIFE TRYING TO CREATE A PROLETARIAN PHILOSOPHY...

It's got to be materialist and dialectical...

"JUST AS PHILOSOPHY FINDS ITS <u>MATERIAL</u> WEAPONS IN THE PROLETARIAT, SO THE PROLETARIAT FINDS ITS <u>INTELLECTUAL</u> WEAPONS IN PHILOSOPHY... PHILOSOPHY CAN ONLY BE REALISED BY THE ABOLITION OF THE PROLETARIAT, AND THE PROLETARIAT CAN ONLY BE ABOLISHED BY THE REALISATION OF PHILOSOPHY."

("Critique of Hegal's Philosophy of Right."
1844)

BUT THE PRIMARY NECESSITY WAS TO KNOW WHAT THE PROLETARIAT THOUGHT, TO LIVE AMONG THEM FOR THE PURPOSE OF UNITING THEORY AND PRACTICE ... AND THE COUNTRY IN WHICH REVOLUTIONARY PRACTICE HAD MADE MOST PROGRESS WAS

France,

THE BIRTHPLACE IN 1789 OF THE FIRST GREAT REVOLUTION IN HUMAN HISTORY, THE

AS WE'VE ALREADY SEEN (BUT PROBABLY FORGOTTEN), MARXISM HAS <u>THREE</u> BASIC SOURCES WHICH ARE:

GERMAN PHILOSOPHY

ENGLISH POLITICAL ECONOMY

FRENCH SOCIALISM

SINCE WE'VE HAD A LOOK AT THE PHILOSOPHICAL ORIGINS, LET'S GLANCE BRIEFLY AT FRENCH SOCIALISM, STARTING WITH:

GRACCHUS BABEUF (PLEASED...)

1760
1797

WHEN THE FRENCH REVOLUTION HAD BEEN DEFEATED, AND THE WORTHY JACOBINS WERE IN RETREAT, A SMALL GROUP OF THEM KNOWN AS

THE 'CONSPIRACY OF EQUALS'

HOPED TO CARRY ON THE ARMED STRUGGLE FOR POWER AND THE CREATION OF A SOCIALIST STATE...

What kind of socialism did they have in mind?

WELL, IT'S NOT KNOWN EXACTLY, BUT, FIRST, THE EXPROPRIATION OF WEALTH AND ITS EQUAL REDISTRIBUTION, THE ESTABLISH- MENT OF <u>COMMON</u> OWNERSHIP. WORK AND EDUCATION COMPULSORY FOR EVERYONE. BUT THE CONSPIRACY WAS DISCOVERED AND BABEUF CONDEMNED...

THE NEXT ATTEMPTS AT SOCIALISM ALSO OCCUR IN FRANCE, DURING NAPOLEON'S REGIME, BUT THESE ATTEMPTS WERE ONLY THEORETICAL.

THE BIG NAMES HERE ARE

SAINT-SIMON
&
FOURIER

KNOWN AS "UTOPIAN SOCIALISTS" BECAUSE WHAT THEY WANTED TO ACHIEVE SEEMED "UTOPIAN" OR "IDEALLY PERFECT"...

...planned economy under the direction of a central bank

...end the rule of the leisure class (nobles, clergy and military)

...organise a new society directed by industrialists to promote the welfare of the larger and poorer classes

...found a new religion which recognises work as man's only merit

SAINT SIMON

WHEN SAINT-SIMON DIED, HIS DISCIPLES REALLY STARTED A RELIGION WITH ITS OWN LITURGY, RITES AND THINGS OF THAT SORT. SAINT-SIMON'S THEORY HAD NO SCIENTIFIC BASIS AT ALL AND IT DID NOT ACKNOWLEDGE THE CLASS STRUGGLE...

Religious morality suffices to eliminate social inequalities...

Fourier

UNLIKE THE ARISTOCRATIC SAINT-SIMON, HE WAS POOR AND SPENT HIS LIFE TRYING TO GET THE RICH TO FINANCE HIS PROJECTS...

He must be mad! Imagine asking the rich to finance their own ruin!

What's he up to, the simpleton??

Oh! not much! He only wants to build a "communist" system of little communities, in which everything belongs to everyone, with communal homes and consumers' co-operatives. To prevent the rise of wealth in any one sector, the richer would get a smaller part of the share, while the poorer got more, (and thereby balance things out). He actually founded a few such communities (called "Phalanstères"). But he spent his last days in a mad-house...

❊ THERE'S NO DOUBT THAT A FEW OF HIS IDEAS MERIT SOME CONSIDERATION. FOR EXAMPLE, THE ELIMINATION OF COMPETITION AMONG PRODUCERS TO STOP THEM CHURNING OUT USELESS THINGS, DUPLICATES AND LUXURY ITEMS...

SOME OF THE IDEAS OF SAINT-SIMON AND FOURIER WERE PROBABLY TAKEN UP BY MARX (AND LENIN!) IN THEIR OWN, MORE PRACTICAL THEORIES.

BUT THE BIGGEST CONTRIBUTION CAME FROM THREE OTHER FRENCH "SOCIALISTS"...

BLANQUI, PROUDHON, AND BLANC

LOUIS-AUGUSTE BLANQUI (1805 – 1881)

*

(sorry! I couldn't find his picture...)

A partisan of class war and armed revolution who spent 33 years of his life in gaol. He first spoke of the Dictatorship of the Proletariat, even if it was a minority one, and not as Marx argued, in the majority...

Anarchist and syndicalist, but despite this, anti-feminist and an avowed enemy of woman's liberation from domestic slavery. He was the founder of mutual aid societies.
"Property is theft."

PROUDHON
1809–1865

Workers' leader, theorist of election-based, legislative socialism, not the violent revolutionary kind.
His most famous saying is:
"From each according to his ability, to each according to his need."

BLANC

1811
1882

MARX CAME INTO CONTACT WITH THEM IN PARIS, OFTEN
STRIVING TO SHOW THEM THEIR ERRORS. SOME WERE FISHING IN
THE TROUBLED WATER OF ADVENTURISM. OTHERS DIDN'T GRASP
MARX'S THEORY AND CALLED IT "UNREALISTIC FOLLY" OR
"EXCESSIVELY RADICAL"...

> This Marx is a proper lunatic! We'll all be senile before his preaching comes to anything..!

BASICALLY, THE ERROR
OF THESE "UTOPIAN SOCIALISTS"
AND ANARCHISTS WAS AN
ABSENCE OF FORESIGHT,
OF PREPARATION,
A CONTEMPT FOR
STUDY AND SLOW,
BUT METHODICAL
ORGANIZATION,
AND THE DENIAL
OF A THEORY OF
HISTORICAL
DEVELOPMENT
THROUGH CLASS
CONFLICT...

> They haven't grasped the class struggle! They imagine society's one big, happy family...

FAMILY??

A HOLY FAMILY??

Hmmmm...

SO MARX HAD SOMETHING NEW TO
ADD TO HIS PARIS "MANUSCRIPTS",
ANOTHER STUDY WITH THE STRANGE TITLE:

THE HOLY FAMILY

Die heilige Familie,

oder

Kritik

der

kritischen Kritik.

Gegen Bruno Bauer & Consorten.

Von

Friedrich Engels und Karl Marx.

Or:
"Critique of Critical Critique. Against Bruno Bauer & Co."

IN THIS BOOK, WRITTEN
WITH ENGELS, MARX
BRINGS TO LIGHT THE
CONFLICT OF CONTRARIES
WHICH GOES ON
WITHIN CAPITALIST
SOCIETY, BETWEEN
CAPITAL AND LABOUR,
THE INEVITABLE
REVOLT OF THE
WORKING CLASS,
AND THE
SUBSEQUENT
DEFEAT OF THE
BOURGEOISIE...
IN TWO WORDS:
THE
CLASS
STRUGGLE...

THIS THESIS WAS
OPPOSED
THROUGHOUT
THE WORLD...

INSTEAD OF
CLASS STRUGGLE,
CAPITALISM
WANTS TO
PREACH AN
"ALLIANCE"
FOR
PROGRESS...

THE AMERICAN TWINS.
"United we stand, Divided we fall."

BUT THE CLASS STRUGGLE ISN'T JUST MARX'S INVENTION. IT HAS ALWAYS EXISTED (AND MAYBE ALWAYS WILL) EVER SINCE THE WORLD BEGAN.
(ALTHOUGH MARX TELLS US IT WON'T <u>ALWAYS</u> EXIST, AS WE SHALL SEE...)

In Rome we have patricians, knights, plebeians and *slaves*...

In the middle Ages; feudal lords, vassals, master artisans, apprentices, serfs...

"THE MODERN BOURGEOIS SOCIETY THAT HAS SPROUTED FROM THE RUINS OF FEUDAL SOCIETY, HAS NOT DONE AWAY WITH CLASS ANTAGONISM. IT HAS BUT ESTABLISHED NEW CLASSES, NEW CONDITIONS OF OPPRESSION, NEW FORMS OF STRUGGLE. ... SOCIETY AS A WHOLE IS MORE AND MORE SPLITTING INTO TWO GREAT HOSTILE CAMPS:

BOURGEOISIE AND PROLETARIAT..."

(That was written in the <u>Manifesto</u> of 1848. But don't go believing Marx was wrong. His epoch was very different from ours...)

WHAT'S IMPORTANT, IS TO GRASP THAT EACH SOCIAL CLASS HAS ITS OWN INTERESTS AND EACH HOLDS VIEWS ABOUT THE GOVERNMENT OF THE STATE CONSISTENT WITH THE DEFENCE OF THOSE INTERESTS...

Social harmony which certain "beautiful souls" preach, CANNOT exist...

He never denied what he owed to others—as in this letter to Weydemeyer, dated March 5, 1852:
'And now as to myself, no credit is due to me for discovering the existence of classes in modern society, nor yet the struggle between them. Long before me, bourgeois historians had described the historical development of this class struggle and bourgeois economists the economic anatomy of the classes. What I did that was new was to prove: 1) that the *existence of classes* is only bound up with *particular, historical phases in the development of production;* 2) that the class struggle necessarily leads to the *dictatorship of the proletariat;* 3) that this dictatorship itself only constitutes the transition to the *abolition of all classes* and to *a classless society."*

IT CAN'T, BECAUSE SO LONG AS ANY ONE CLASS LIVES BY EXPLOITING ANOTHER, A STRUGGLE WILL EXIST AGAINST SUCH EXPLOITATION...

And this class struggle is NECESSARY for human progress...

93

IT'S NOT ON BECAUSE THE CAPITALIST SYSTEM HAS ONLY ONE AIM, <u>PROFIT</u>, BASED ON <u>PRIVATE PROPERTY</u>, WHICH IS OBTAINED BY <u>EXPLOITING</u> THE LABOURS OF THE PROLETARIAT...

MARX PROVES WITH GREAT PRECISION THAT UNDER THIS "NEW SYSTEM", (CAPITALISM, THAT IS) THE WORKER IS CONDEMNED NEVER TO ENJOY THE ADVANTAGES WHICH THE SYSTEM RESERVES ONLY FOR THE <u>OWNERS</u> OF THE MEANS OF PRODUCTION...

> Who ends up with the profits that you produce?

> Who else but the boss, that's who!...

AND WHY <u>ONLY</u> THE BOSS?

SO MARX HAD TO SWITCH FROM PHILOSOPHICAL PROBLEMS TO THOSE WHICH PHILOSOPHY USUALLY IGNORES, BUT HE RECKONED THAT IT WAS NECESSARY TO COME TO GRIPS WITH THEM BEFORE HE COULD PROVE HIS THEORIES:

ECONOMIC PROBLEMS

> His own, maybe?

THE PECULIAR MR. MARX WHO NEVER MANAGED TO SOLVE HIS OWN FINANCIAL PROBLEMS (HIS FAMILY OFTEN WENT HUNGRY) WANTS TO RESOLVE THE PROBLEMS OF MILLIONS OF EXPLOITED WORKERS; IN LONDON, PARIS, ROME, BERLIN, BRUSSELS,

I COULD GO ON ALL DAY...

95

MARX WAS BY NOW LIVING IN THE DEEPEST POVERTY, WITHOUT SALARY AND WITHOUT CAPITAL...

Except the one he was writing!

BUT IT'S EASIER TO UNDERSTAND HIM BY QUOTING FROM A LETTER THAT HE WROTE TO HIS OLD FRIEND ENGELS...

Marx to Engels, Sept. 8, 1852.

"You will have seen from my letters that, as usual when I am right in the shit myself and not merely hearing about it from a distance, I show complete indifference. Anyway, *que faire?* My house is a hospital and the crisis is so disrupting that it requires all my attention . . . The atmosphere is very disturbed: my wife is ill, Jennychen is ill and Lenchen has a kind of nervous fever. I couldn't and can't call the doctor, because I have no money for the medicine. For eight or ten days I have managed to feed the family on bread and potatoes, but it is still doubtful whether I can get hold of any today. . . I have written no articles for Dana because I had not a penny to go and read the newspaper. . . Besides there is the baker, milkman, greengrocer, and old butcher's bills. How can I deal with all this devilish filth? And then finally, during the last eight or ten days I managed to borrow a few shillings and pence which were absolutely necessary if we were to avoid giving up the ghost. . ."

WAGES PRICES
CAPITAL PROFITS
VALUE
RAW MATERIALS
THE HOLY EUCHARIST!

MARX BEGINS:
WHAT IS SALARY?

HOW IS IT DEFINED?

If workers were asked: "How much are your wages?" one would reply: "I get a mark a day from my bourgeois," another "I get two marks," and so on. According to the different trades to which they belong, they would mention different sums of money which they receive from their respective bourgeois for a particular period of labour or for the completion of a particular piece of work, e.g. weaving a yard of linen or type-setting a printed sheet. In spite of the variety of their statements, they would all agree on one point: wages are the sum of money paid by the capitalist for a particular period of labour or for a particular output of labour.

The capitalist, it appears, therefore *buys* their labour with money. They *sell* him their labour for money. But this is merely the appearance. In reality what they sell to the capitalist is their labour *power*. The capitalist buys this labour power for a day, a week, a month, etc. And after he has bought it, he uses it by having the workers work for the stipulated time. For the same sum with which the capitalist has bought their labour power, e.g. two marks, he could have bought two pounds of sugar or a definite amount of any other commodity. The two marks, with which he bought two pounds of sugar, are the *price* of the two pounds of sugar. The two marks, with which he bought twelve hours' use of labour power, are the price of twelve hours' labour. Labour power, therefore, is a commodity, neither more nor less than sugar. The former is measured by the clock, the latter by the scales.

(Marx, *Wage-Labour and Capital*)

HAVE YOU UNDERSTOOD?
THE WORKER EXCHANGES HIS COMMODITY
(LABOUR-POWER) FOR AN EQUIVALENT WAGE
(SO THE BOSS SAYS) TO PURCHASE WHAT HE
NEEDS TO SURVIVE: LIGHT, FOOD, ROOF, CLOTHES...

Or rather, just to keep afloat...

BUT IF A WORKER'S PAY WERE CALCULATED ON HIS BASIC NEEDS, IT WOULD HAVE TO BE A VERY GOOD PAY, SO THE BOSSES MIGHT ARGUE...

...But it's not true!

LET'S CHECK THAT AGAINST THE PROFIT MADE FROM A WORKER'S LABOUR. ENGELS, WHO WAS A 'BOSS' HIMSELF, EXPLAINS HOW...

Let us assume that our worker— a machinist—has to make a part of a machine which he can complete in one day. The raw material—iron and brass in the necessary previously prepared form—costs, twenty marks. The consumption of coal by the steam-engine, the wear and tear of this same engine, of the lathe and other tools which our worker uses, represent for one day, and reckoned by his share of their use, a value of one mark. The wage for one day, according to our assumption, is three marks. This makes twenty-four marks in all for our machine part. But the capitalist calculates that he will obtain, on an average, twenty-seven marks from his customers in return, or three marks more than his outlay.

Whence came the three marks pocketed by the capitalist? According to the assertion of classical economics, commodities are, on the average, sold at their values, that is, at prices corres- ponding to the amount of necessary labour contained in them. The average price of our machine part—twenty-seven marks— would thus be equal to its value, that is equal to the labour embodied in it. But of these twenty-seven marks, twenty-one marks were values already present before our machinist began work. Twenty marks were contained in the raw materials, one mark in the coal consumed during the work, or in the machines and tools which were used in the process and which were diminished in their efficiency to the value of this sum. There remain six marks which have been added to the value of the raw material. But according to the assumption of our economists themselves, these six marks can only arise from the labour added to the raw material by our worker. His twelve hours' labour has thus created a new value of six marks. The value of his twelve hours' labour would, therefore, be equal to six marks. And thereby we would at last have discovered what the "value of labour" is.

(Engels, *Wage-Labour and Capital*)

Six marks? But I only get three!!

Yeah, so do I!

... IN OTHER WORDS, THE OWNER MAKES IN A DAY WHAT <u>ALL</u> THE WORKERS PUT TOGETHER EARN, <u>AND</u> WITHOUT DIRTYING HIS HANDS, MILORD! ...

Yes, but I put up the <u>money</u>!

IT GOES WITHOUT SAYING— THE WORKER WORKS TO LIVE. WHAT HE EARNS GOES INTO KEEPING HIS FAMILY ALIVE, AND SO HE PASSES THE BEST YEARS OF HIS LIFE DOING WHAT HE DOESN'T LIKE DOING... WHILE THE BOSS GROWS RICHER AND RICHER...

WHILE THE BOSSES RUN TO CONSULT THEIR ECONOMISTS AND IDEOLOGISTS, HOPING TO FIND SOME WAY TO COMBAT HIS THEORIES, MARX CONTINUES: "SALARY IS THE PRICE OF A GIVEN COMMODITY... BUT HOW IS THE PRICE OF A COMMODITY DETERMINED?"...

99

WHAT DETERMINES THE PRICE OF ANY PRODUCT IS COMPETITION, OR, MORE EXACTLY, THREE KINDS OF COMPETITION:

SELLER VERSUS SELLER

PURCHASER VERSUS PURCHASER

SELLER VERSUS PURCHASER

WHEN SEVERAL VENDORS HAVE THE SAME MERCHANDISE TO SELL, THEY BECOME COMPETITORS WHO MAY RESORT TO CUT-PRICE TACTICS...

This LOWERS prices

WHEN A NUMBER OF PURCHASERS HEAD FOR THE SAME COMMODITY, IT GOES TO ONE WHO'S WILLING TO PAY MORE FOR IT...

This RAISES prices

COMPETITION BETWEEN SELLER AND BUYER OCCURS WHEN ONE WANTS TO SELL HIGH, AND THE OTHER WANTS TO BUY CHEAP...

Here everything depends on the previous competition!

That's the law of "supply and demand", kiddo!!

WHEN THERE ARE 100 CARS AND 1000 POSSIBLE BUYERS, THE PRICE OF THE VEHICLE JUMPS UP ACCORDING TO THE WISHES OF THE SELLER... BUT IF THERE ARE 100 CARS AND ONLY 20 BUYERS, IT'S VERY PROBABLE THE PRICE WILL FAVOUR THE BUYER...

But we still don't know what it is that determines prices...

LET'S TALK ABOUT THE PRICE OF PRODUCTION... AN AUTOMOBILE, FOR INSTANCE, JUST OFF THE ASSEMBLY LINE COSTS £10,000; ADD TO THIS ALL THE HIDDEN COSTS SUCH AS PUBLICITY, PUBLIC RELATIONS EXERCISES, THE DISTRIBUTOR'S PERCENTAGE, TAXES, THE PRODUCER'S PROFIT...

Result? The retail price to the public jumps to £20,000...

MARX DIDN'T KNOW ABOUT SUCH NOVELTIES AS SALES REPRESENTATIVES, P.R. AND AD. MEN, ALL OF **WHOM** GROSSLY **INFLATE** THE PRICE OF GOODS...

...I'd have given 'em a whole chapter in my 'Capital'

ANYWAY, THE QUESTION HAS BEEN ASKED WHETHER (AND BY HOW MUCH) THE PROFITS OF THE WEALTHY MIGHT BE LIMITED... BY 10%? IS THAT "FAIR AND DECENT"? BUT AT THIS RATE, THE PROBLEM CAN NEVER BE RESOLVED...

(Some businesses function at 200% profit...) So???

SO IT'S THE LABOUR-POWER OF THE WORKER WHICH DAY BY DAY SWELLS THE BOSS'S CAPITAL. THE RICH BECOME EVEN RICHER, WHILE THE POOR CERTAINLY DON'T GET ANY FATTER ON THEIR WAGES (WHICH HARDLY KEEP PACE...)

The world is all upside-down...!!

WHILE THE BOSS, THE CAPITALIST AND THE RICH MAN MAKE A FABULOUS PROFIT FROM THE WORKER'S LABOUR, THE POOR FELLOW DOESN'T MAKE A PENNY EXTRA FOR HIS WORK...

THIS DRAWING ⬆ SHOWS THE PROCESS AT WORK: THE INPUTS OF THE CAPITALIST AND THE WORKER (MONEY FROM ONE AND LABOUR FROM THE OTHER) COMING TOGETHER TO CREATE A PRODUCT.

BUT THE PROFIT FLOWS ONLY IN ONE DIRECTION, NOT BOTH, AS JUSTICE DEMANDS...

SO ONE GROWS FAT WHILE THE OTHER TIGHTENS WHAT'S LEFT OF HIS BELT...

SURPLUS VALUE

I promise not to yawn if you keep it simple...

O.K. LET'S PROCEED. THE BASIC FORMULA OF CAPITALISM IS VERY SIMPLE: BUYING SO AS TO SELL AGAIN FOR PROFIT. THIS INCREASE IN THE VALUE OF THE MONEY EMPLOYED WHICH RESULTS FROM THE TRANSACTION, MARX CALLS SURPLUS VALUE.

MARX REASONED THUS: SURPLUS VALUE CANNOT DERIVE FROM THE MERE EXCHANGE OF GOODS, SINCE THIS IS AN EXCHANGE OF EQUIVALENT THINGS, COMMODITIES ARE SOLD TO BUY OTHER COMMODITIES...

... EVEN LESS DOES SURPLUS VALUE COME FROM INCREASES OF PRICE, SINCE THE RECIPROCAL PROFIT-AND-LOSS BETWEEN BUYERS AND SELLERS TENDS TO BALANCE OUT...

If one gains, the other loses!

WELL THEN!

TO OBTAIN SURPLUS VALUE (EXTRA PROFIT), THE POSSESSOR OF CASH HAS GOT TO FIND ON THE MARKET SOME OTHER "COMMODITY" WITH THE CURRENT VALUE HAVING THE ONE PECULIAR QUALITY WHICH MAKES IT THE <u>SOURCE OF VALUE</u>...

Simple! Human labour-power!

THE CAPITALIST BUYS THE WORKER'S LABOUR-POWER AS IF IT WAS ANY OTHER KIND OF MERCHANDISE, AND PUTS IT TO WORK EIGHT HOURS A DAY (IN MARX'S TIME, THE WORKING DAY WAS <u>12 TO 15 HOURS</u>...)

Gosh! and what is that commodity?

But the worker can make, say, in 6 hours ("necessary" working time) a product which is enough for his livelihood

This surplus product, the boss's extra profit, is surplus value...

In six hours he "produces his salary"...

THANKS TO SURPLUS VALUE, THE BOSS GETS RICHER, WHILE THE WORKER EARNS NOT A PENNY FROM IT. SURE, SOME MONEY IS SUPPOSED TO BE USED TO IMPROVE WORKING CONDITIONS... BUT IT GOES STRAIGHT INTO THE BANK...

To fatten my capital some more...

In the two hours remaining he produces another commodity, a "surplus" product for which his boss doesn't pay him anything...

THIS IS THE TRAP OF PRESENT-DAY CAPITALISM: INCREASING THE WORKER'S PRODUCTIVE OUTPUT AND HIS EFFICIENCY, ALSO INCREASES SURPLUS VALUE...

A RISE IN PRODUCTIVITY IS NOTHING OTHER THAN A WAY TO AUGMENT THE BOSS'S CAPITAL — AND THE POVERTY OF ALL WORKERS...!!

MARX DIDN'T AGREE WITH THIS BECAUSE...

WELL, JUST READ WHAT HE THOUGHT...

Real wages may remain the same, they may even rise, and yet relative wages fall. Let us suppose, for example, that all means of subsistence have gone down in price by two-thirds while wages per day have only fallen by one-third, that is to say, for example, from three marks to two marks. Although the worker can command a greater amount of commodities with these two marks than he previously could with three marks, yet his wages have gone down in relation to the profit of the capitalist. The profit of the capitalist (e.g. the manufacturer) has increased by one mark, that is, for a smaller sum of exchange values which he pays to the worker, the latter must produce a greater amount of exchange values than before. The share of capital relative to the share of labour has risen. The division of social wealth between capital and labour has become still more unequal. With the same capital, the capitalist commands a greater quantity of labour. The power of the capitalist class over the working class has grown, the social position of the worker has deteriorated, has been depressed one stage further below that of the capitalist. *What then is the general law which determines the rise and fall of wages and profits in their reciprocal relation?*

They stand in inverse ratio to each other. Capital's share, profit, rises in the same proportion as labour's share, wages, falls and vice versa. Profit rises to the extent that wages fall; it falls to the extent that wages rise.

(Marx, *Wage-Labour and Capital*)

(WHICH MEANS: THE BOSS NEVER WANTS TO LOSE...)

TAKE THE EXAMPLE OF CONSTRUCTION:

What've I got to do with it?

WELL, BY BUILDING APARTMENT BLOCKS IN WHICH YOU'LL NEVER LIVE AND FROM WHICH YOU'LL NEVER COLLECT RENT, YOU'RE ONLY HELPING THE CLASS WHICH EXPLOITS YOU TO GROW RICHER....

EVEN BY EARNING MORE — INDEED, DOUBLE — THE WORKER'S SITUATION WON'T CHANGE. MARX SAYS IT CLEARLY:

The best salary workers can get, under the most favourable conditions, only reveals in reality the strength and thickness of the golden bars which imprison them, and which only seem to permit them "greater" freedom of action...

* MORE SALARY, MORE PROFIT FOR THE BOSS...

Hang on! That's not from Marx

(You're right! An Austrian Marxist, Ernst Fischer, said it, and he goes on...)

"...THE MISERY OF THE WORKER, ABOVE ALL, CONSISTS OF THE FACT THAT BY WORKING FOR CAPITALISM HE REPRODUCES CAPITAL, AND BY REPRODUCING IT, HE ALSO INCREASES HIS OWN ALIENATION AND MISERY..."

By 'eck! and what do I do then?

107

MARX SEES ONLY ONE WAY OUT FOR THE WORKERS:

UNION

Union with THE Bosses?

(WELL, WELL! A SCAB!) LET'S GO BACK IN TIME TO THE PERIOD WHEN MARX SET OUT HIS THEORIES ON THE TRANSFORMATION OF SOCIETY AND THE LIBERATION OF THE POOR FROM THEIR CHAINS...
(Gold, silver or tin...)

The historic moment is THE publication of the COMMUNIST MANIFESTO

What?? Communist Parties didn't exist already?

The *Manifesto* was published as the platform of the Communist League, a workingmen's association, first exclusively German, later on international, and, under the political conditions of the Continent before 1848, unavoidably a secret society. At a Congress of the League, held in London in November 1847, Marx and Engels were commissioned to prepare for publication a complete theoretical and practical party program. Drawn up in German, in January 1848, the manuscript was sent to the printer in London a few weeks before the French revolution of February 24th. A French translation was brought out in Paris, shortly before the insurrection of June 1848. The first English translation, by Miss Helen Macfarlane, appeared in the *Red Republican*, London, 1850. A Danish and a Polish edition had also been published. . . The first Russian translation, made by Bakunin, was published at Herzen's *Kolokol* office in Geneva, about 1863. . .

However much the state of things may have altered during the last 25 years, the general principles laid down in this *Manifesto* are, on the whole, as correct today as ever.
(Engels, 1888 preface to the *Communist Manifesto*)

BACK IN THOSE DAYS (1846-47), THERE WAS A GROUP MADE UP OF GERMAN WORKERS, ARTISANS AND INTELLECTUALS OF THE AVANT-GARDE (I.E. OF ADVANCED IDEAS) CALLING ITSELF THE "LEAGUE OF THE JUST", WHICH MET TO TALK POLITICS AND KEEP IN TOUCH WITH THE "JUST" MEN IN OTHER COUNTRIES...

THE "JUST" WERE HALF ANARCHIST AND PREACHED A PRETTY STRANGE FORM OF SOCIALISM: DESTRUCTION OF THE MEANS OF PRODUCTION (BLOWING UP FACTORIES, PREFERABLY WITH THE BOSSES IN THEM) AND A RETURN TO AGRICULTURE AND ARTISAN CRAFTSMANSHIP... IN FEBRUARY 1847, MARX AND ENGELS WERE INVITED TO JOIN THE LEAGUE TO HELP TO REORGANISE IT..

MARX AND ENGELS IMMEDIATELY GAINED THE LEAGUE'S FULL SYMPATHY, AND THANKS TO THEIR GREATER INTELLECTUAL AND POLITICAL MATURITY, THEY HAD A BIG INFLUENCE OVER THE LEAGUE... MARX, THE "TOUGH GUY" KNEW HOW TO COMMAND...

... to start, instead of the "Just", we'll call ourselves the League of Communists...

Right?...

TOUGH-MINDED GERMANS, AS THEY ALWAYS REMAINED, MARX AND ENGELS ORGANISED A LONDON CONGRESS IN 1847 WHICH BROUGHT IN DELEGATES FROM EVERY CORNER OF EUROPE.
AND HERE, ENGELS PROPOSED HIS "<u>CREDOS</u>" OF THE COMMUNIST LEAGUE WHICH SERVED AS THE PLATFORM OF THE "COMMUNIST MANIFESTO"....
(ALSO KNOWN AS THE "PRINCIPLES OF COMMUNISM", 1847)

Question 1: *What is communism?*
Answer: Communism is the doctrine of the prerequisites for the emancipation of the proletariat.

Question 2: *What is the proletariat?*
Answer: The proletariat is that class of society whose means of livelihood entirely depend on the sale of its labor and not on the profit derived from capital; whose weal and woe, whose life and death, whose whole existence depend on the demand for labor, hence on the alternation of good times and bad, on the vagaries of unbridled competition. The proletariat, or class of proletarians, is, in a word, the working class of the 19th century.

Question 3: *Proletarians, then, have not always existed?*
Answer: No. Poor folk and working classes have always existed. The working classes have also for the most part been poor. But such poor, such workers as are living under conditions indicated above, hence proletarians, have not always existed, any more than free and unbridled competition has always existed.

Question 4: *How did the proletariat originate?*
Answer: The proletariat originated in the industrial revolution which took place in England during the second half of the 18th century and which has repeated itself since then in all the civilized countries of the world. This industrial revolution took place owing to the invention of the steam engine, of various spinning machines, of the power loom, and of a great number of other mechanical instruments. These machines were expensive and, consequently, could only be installed by persons who had plenty of capital to lay out. Their introduction completely altered the existing method of production and displaced the existing workers. This was due to the fact that machinery could produce cheaper and better commodities than could the handi-craftsmen with their imperfect spinning wheels and hand looms. Thus, these machines handed over industry entirely to the big capitalists and rendered the little property the workers possessed (tools, hand looms, etc.) entirely worthless. Soon the capitalists got all in their hands and nothing remained for the workers.

NOTE: THIS KIND OF EASY-TO-READ CATECHISM STYLE MADE ENGELS MORE POPULAR THAN MARX, WHO, DEEPER AS HE WAS, SEEMED PRETTY HARD TO DIGEST...

Question 7: *In what way does the proletarian differ from the slave?*

Answer: The slave is sold once and for all. The proletarian must sell himself by the hour or by the day. Each individual slave, being the direct property of a master, has his existence assured, be that existence ever so wretched, if only because of the interest of the slave owner. Each individual proletarian, the property as it were of the whole bourgeois *class,* whose labor is sold only when it is needed by the owning class, has no security of life. Existence is merely guaranteed to the working *class* as a whole. The slave is excluded from competition; the proletarian is beset by competition and is a prey to all its fluctuations. The slave is counted an object and not a member of civil society; the proletarian is recognized as a person, as a member of civil society. The slave may therefore be able to secure better conditions of life than can the proletarian, but the proletarian belongs to a higher stage of development of society than the slave. The slave frees himself by rupturing, of all relations of private ownership, only one, the relation of slavery and by this act becomes himself a proletarian; the proletarian can only achieve emancipation by abolishing private property in its entirety.

If what he says is true, we're cooked!

CHILE

Question 16: *Will it be possible to bring about the abolition of private property by peaceful methods?*

Answer: This is greatly to be desired, and communists would be the last persons in the world to stand in the way of a peaceful solution. Communists know only too well the futility and, indeed, the harmfulness of conspiratorial methods. They know only too well that revolutions are not made deliberately and arbitrarily, but that everywhere and at all times revolutions have been the necessary outcome of circumstances quite independent of the will or the guidance of particular parties and whole classes. But they also perceive that the development of the proletariat in nearly all civilized countries is violently suppressed, and that in this way opponents of communism are working full force to promote a revolution. Should the oppressed proletariat at long last thus be driven into a revolution, then we communists will rally to the cause of the workers and be just as prompt to act as we are now to speak.

111

Question 17: *Will it be possible to abolish private property all at once?*

Answer: No. This would be just as impossible as to multiply all at once the existing forces of production to the degree necessary for the inauguration of the community. The proletarian revolution, which in all probability is coming, will for this reason, only be able to transform present society gradually. Private property will be abolished only when the means of production have become available in sufficient quantities.

FIRST LONDON EDITION, FERUARY 1848, OF THE

COMMUNIST MANIFESTO

Print-run? Only 1000 copies

Published in German, English, French, Russian and Spanish...

Authors? Monx and Engels

... and then in Italian, Danish, Swedish, Flemish, Chinese, Czech, Hungarian,... In... Arf! Arf!

The *Manifesto* is a direct appeal to all workers—*Workers of the World, unite*! It defends the Communist position that the emancipation of the working class itself must be the act of the working class itself. Its lucid, powerful arguments are still potent today. It moves us to take a definite position against the structure of a society in which the unjust division of wealth contradicts basic decency.

Modern industry has established the world market, for which the discovery of America paved the way. This market has given an immense development to commerce, to navigation, to communication by land. This development has, in its turn, reacted on the extension of industry; and in proportion as industry, commerce, navigation, railways extended, in the same proportion the bourgeoisie developed, increased its capital, and pushed into the background every class handed down from the Middle Ages.

THE MANIFESTO IS REALLY AN AMALGAMATION OF MARX'S IDEAS WRITTEN IN A RICH, LIVELY AND DIRECT STYLE...

Read it and you'll see for yourself!

We quote only parts of it, or it would take up ½ the book...

We see, therefore, how the modern bourgeoisie is itself the product of a long course of development, of a series of revolutions in the modes of production and of exchange. The bourgeoisie, wherever it has got the upper hand, has put an end to all feudal, patriarchal, idyllic relations. It has pitilessly torn asunder the motley feudal ties that bound man to his "natural superiors", and has left remaining no other nexus between man and man than naked self-interest, than callous "cash payment". It has drowned the most heavenly ecstasies of religious fervour, of chivalrous enthusiasm, of philistine sentimentalism, in the icy water of egotistical calculation. It has resolved personal worth into exchange value, and in place of the numberless indefeasible chartered freedoms, has set up that single, unconscionable freedom—Free Trade. In one word, for exploitation, veiled by religious and political illusions, it has substituted naked, shameless, direct, brutal exploitation. The bourgeoisie has born away from the family its sentimental veil, and has reduced the family relation to a mere money relation.

What you have is what you're worth...

The bourgeoisie, during its rule of scarce one hundred years, has created more massive and more colossal productive forces than have all preceding generations together. Subjection of Nature's forces to man, machinery, application of chemistry to industry and agriculture, steam-navigation, railways, electric telegraphs, clearing of whole continents for cultivation, canalisation of rivers, whole populations conjured out of the ground—what earlier century had even a presentiment that such productive forces slumbered in the lap of social labour?

Owing to the extensive use of machinery and to division of labour, the work of the proletarians has lost all individual character, and, consequently, all charm for the workman. He becomes an appendage of the machine, and it is only the most simple, most monotonous, and most easily acquired knack, that is required of him. Hence, the cost of production of a workman is restricted, almost entirely, to the means of subsistence that he requires for his maintenance, and for the propagation of his race. But the price of a commodity, and therefore also of labour, is equal to its cost of production. In proportion, therefore, as the repulsiveness of the work increases, the wage decreases.

But Big Mama Television wasn't around yet to stupefy us all the more before going to bed...

Modern industry has converted the little workshop of the patriarchal master into the great factory of the industrial capitalist. Masses of labourers, crowded into the factory, are organised like soldiers. As privates of the industrial army they are placed under the command of a perfect hierarchy of officers and sergeants. Not only are they slaves of the bourgeois class, and of the bourgeois State; they are daily and hourly enslaved by the machine, by the over-looker, and, above all, by the individual bourgeois manufacturer himself. The more openly this depotism proclaims gain to be its end and aim, the more petty, the more hateful and the more embittered it is.

The less the skill and exertion of strength implied in manual labour, in other words, the more modern industry becomes developed, the more is the labour of men superseded by that of women. Differences of age and sex have no longer any distinctive social validity for the working class. All are instruments of labour, more or less expensive to use, according to their age and sex.

No sooner is the exploitation of the labourer by the manufacturer, so far, at an end, that he receives his wages in cash, than he is set upon by the other portions of the bourgeoisie, the landlord, the shopkeeper, the pawnbroker, etc.

But with the development of industry the proletariat not only increases in number; it becomes concentrated in greater masses, its strength grows, and it feels that strength more. The various interests and conditions of life within the ranks of the proletariat are more and more equalised, in proportion as machinery obliterates all distinctions of labour, and nearly everywhere reduces wages to the same low level. The growing competition among the bourgeois, and the resulting commercial crises, make the wages of the workers ever more fluctuating. The unceasing improvement of machinery, ever more rapidly developing, makes their livelihood more and more precarious; the collisions between individual workmen and individual bourgeois take more and more the character of collisions between two classes. Thereupon the workers begin to form combinations (Trades' Unions) against the bourgeois; they club together in order to keep up the rate of wages; they found permanent associations in order to make provision beforehand for these occasional revolts. Here and there the contest breaks out into riots.

... And here's how Marx formulates the class struggle ...

Now and then the workers are victorious, but only for a time. The real fruit of their battles lies, not in the immediate result, but in the ever-expanding union of the workers. This union is helped on by the improved means of communication that are created by modern industry and that place the workers of different localities in contact with one another. It was just this contact that was needed to centralise the numerous local struggles, all of the same character, into one national struggle between classes. But every class struggle is a political struggle. And that union, to attain which the burghers of the Middle Ages, with their miserable highways, required centuries, the modern proletarians, thanks to railways, achieve in a few years. This organisation of the proletarians into a class, and consequently into a political party, is continually being upset again by the competition between the workers themselves. But it ever rises up again, stronger, firmer, mightier. It compels legislative recognition of particular interests of the workers, by taking advantage of the divisions among the bourgeoisie itself. Thus the ten-hours' bill in England was carried.

And what says this Manifesto about the down-and-out?

Of all the classes that stand face to face with the bourgeoisie today, the proletariat alone is a really revolutionary class. The other classes decay and finally disappear in the face of modern industry; the proletariat is its special and essential product.
The lower middle class, the small manufacturer, the shopkeeper, the artisan, the peasant, all these fight against the bourgeoisie, to save from extinction their existence as fractions of the middle class. They are therefore not revolutionary, but conservative. Nay more, they are reactionary, for they try to roll back the wheel of history. If by chance they are revolutionary, they are so only in view of their impending transfer into the proletariat, they thus defend not their present, but their future interests, they desert their own standpoint to place themselves at that of the proletariat.
The "dangerous class", the social scum, that passively rotting mass thrown off by the lowest layers of old society, may, here and there, be swept into the movement by a proletarian revolution; its conditions of life, however, prepare it far more for the part of a bribed tool of reactionary intrigue.

Just like scabs...

All property relations in the past have continually been subject to historical change consequent upon the change in historical conditions.

The French Revolution, for example, abolished feudal property in favour of bourgeois property.

The distinguishing feature of Communism is not the abolition of property generally, but the abolition bourgeois property. But modern bourgeois private property is the final and most complete expression of the system of producing and appropriating products, that is based on class antagonisms, on the exploitation of the many by the few.

In this sense, the theory of the Communists may be summed up in the single sentence: Abolition of private property.

We Communists have been reproached with the desire of abolishing the right of personally acquiring property as the fruit of a man's own labour, which property is alleged to be the ground work of all personal freedom, activity and independence.

Hard-won, self-acquired, self-earned property! Do you mean the property of the petty artisan and of the small peasant, a form of property that preceded the bourgeois form? There is no need to abolish that; the development of industry has to a great extent already destroyed it, and is still destroying it daily.

Or do you mean modern bourgeois private property?

But does wage labour create any property for the labourer? Not a bit. It creates capital, i.e. that kind of property which exploits wage labour, and which cannot increase except upon condition of begetting a new supply of wage labour for fresh exploitation. Property, in its present form, is based on the antagonism of capital and wage labour. Let us examine both sides of this antagonism.

You are horrified at our intending to do away with private property. But in your existing society, private property is already done away with for nine-tenths of the population; its existence for the few is solely due to its non-existence in the hands of those nine-tenths. You reproach us, therefore, with intending to do away with a form of property, the necessary condition for whose existence is, the non-existence of any property for the immense majority of society.

BUT THE WORLD WOULD GO TO RACK AND RUIN
OR SO THEY SAY...

In one word, you reproach us with intending to do away with your property. Precisely so; that is just what we intend.
From the moment when labour can no longer be converted into capital, money, or rent, into a social power capable of being monopolised, i.e. from the moment when individual property can no longer be transformed into Bourgeois property, into capital, from that moment, you say, individuality vanishes. You must, therefore, confess that by "individual" you mean no other person than the bourgeois, than the middle-class owner of property. This person must, indeed, be swept out of the way, and made impossible.

Capital needs workers, but workers don't need capital. It's in the strength of their arms...!

It has been objected that upon the abolition of private property all work will cease, and universal laziness will overtake us. According to this, bourgeois society ought long ago to have gone to the dogs through sheer idleness; for those of its members who work, acquire nothing, and those who acquire anything, do not work. The whole of this objection is but another expression of the tautology: that there can no longer be any wage-labour when there is no longer any capital.

The bourgeois sees in his wife a mere instrument of production. He hears that the instruments of production are to be exploited in common, and, naturally, can come to no other conclusion than that the lot of being common to all will likewise fall to the woman.

He has not even a suspicion that the real point aimed at is to do away with the status of women as mere instruments of production.

For the rest, nothing is more ridiculous than the virtuous indignation of our bourgeois at the community of women which, they pretend, is to be openly and officially established by the Communists. The Communists have no need to introduce community of women; it has existed almost from time immemorial.

Our bourgeois, not content with having the wives and daughters of their proletarians at their disposal, not to speak of common prostitutes, take the greatest pleasure in seducing each other's wives.

Bourgeois marriage is in reality a system of wives in common and thus, at the most, what the Communists might possibly be reproached with, is that they desire to introduce, in substitution for a hypocritically concealed, an openly legalised community of women. For the rest, it is self-evident that the abolition of the present system of production must bring with it the abolition of the community of women springing from that system, i.e. of prostitution both public and private.

(And since we're talking about women, let's see what old Prof. Engels had to say...)

Go on! Women's Lib is already 100 years old!!

This situation changed with the patriarchal family and even more with the monogamous individual family. The administration of the household lost its public character. It was no longer the concern of society. It became *private service*. The wife became the first domestic servant, pushed out of participation in social production. Only modern large-scale industry again threw open to her — and only to the proletarian woman at that — the avenue to social production; but in such a way that, when she fulfils her duties in the private service of her family, she remains excluded from public production and cannot earn anything; and when she wishes to take part in public industry and earn her living independently, she is not in a position to fulfil her family duties. What applies to the woman in the factory applies to her in all professions, right up to medicine and law. The modern individual family is based on the open or disguised domestic enslavement of the woman; and modern society is a mass composed solely of individual families as its molecules. Today, in the great majority of cases, the man has to be the earner, the breadwinner of the family, at least among the propertied classes, and this gives him a dominating position which requires no special legal privileges. In the family, he is the bourgeois; the wife represents the proletariat.

MARX'S PROPHETIC VISION IS PRETTY ASTONISHING.

THAT'S WHY HIS WRITINGS DON'T GO OUT OF DATE.

Blimey! Was that written in 1848 or today??

But let's get on with the Manifesto:

We have seen above, that the first step in the revolution by the working class, is to raise the proletariat to the position of ruling class, to win the battle of democracy.

The proletariat will use its political supremacy to wrest, by degrees, all capital from the bourgeoisie, to centralise all instruments of production in the hands of the State. i.e. of the proletariat organised as the ruling class; and to increase the total of productive forces as rapidly as possible.

Of course, in the beginning, this cannot be effected except by means of despotic inroads on the rights of property, and on the conditions of bourgeois production; by means of measures, therefore, which appear economically insufficient and untenable, but which, in the course of the movement, outstrip themselves, necessitate further inroads upon the old social order, and are unavoidable as a means of entirely revolutionising the mode of production.

These measures will of course be different in different countries.

What are the socialist measures Charlie mentions?

YOU CAN SEE – LISTED BELOW – THE FIRST PRACTICAL PROGRAMME FOR CONSTRUCTING SOCIALISM:...
AND IF YOU COMPARE IT WITH PRESENT-DAY REALITY, TWO THINGS BECOME CLEAR:
① THE INFLUENCE OF MARX EVERYWHERE IN THE WORLD...
AND ② COUNTRIES TODAY (AFTER 120 YEARS) WHICH HAVEN'T YET IMPLEMENTED (AND DON'T FORESEE DOING SO) EVEN THIS MINIMUM AND INCOMPLETE PROGRAMME...

Nevertheless in the most advanced countries, the following will be pretty generally applicable:

1. Abolition of property in land and application of all rents of land to public purposes.

2. A heavy progressive or graduated income tax.

3. Abolition of all right of inheritance.

4. Confiscation of the property of all emigrants and rebels.

5. Centralisation of credit in the hands of the State, by means of a national bank with State capital and an exclusive monopoly.

6. Centralisation of means of communication and transport in the hands of the State.

7. Extension of factories and instruments of production owned by the State; the bringing into cultivation of waste-lands, and the improvement of the soil generally in accordance with a common plan.

8. Equal liability of all to labour. Establishment of industrial armies, especially for agriculture.

9. Combination of agriculture with manufacturing industries; gradual abolition of the distinction between town and country, by a more equable distribution of the population over the country.

10. Free education for all children in public schools. Abolition of children's factory labour in its present form. Combination of education with industrial production, &c., &c.

HERR KARL MARX (ALIAS THE "TOUGH GUY") FORCEFULLY DEMONSTRATES THAT CAPITALISM IS _INCAPABLE_ OF RESOLVING THE PROBLEMS OF HUMANITY. SO LONG AS THE SYSTEM GOES ON DEVELOPING, EVERYTHING WILL GO FROM BAD TO WORSE... A DECADENT EMPIRE SPREADING LIKE A PLAGUE EVERYWHERE...

Is that —gulp— North American Imperialism..?

WHY'S THAT?

What went wrong with the bourgeoisie who'd started off so well?

Why has it produced gangster representatives like Hitler, Trujillo, the Brazilian apes, Truman, Franco, Pinochet, Nixon and the rest...?

MARX COULDN'T MAKE IT ANY PLAINER. ALL SYSTEMS WHICH CARRY THE DESTRUCTIVE SEEDS OF CLASS WAR WILL EVENTUALLY DISAPPEAR... BUT BEFORE GOING UNDER, THEY DEFEND THEMSELVES TO THE DEATH LIKE SAVAGE, WOUNDED BEASTS, UNTIL THE UP-AND-COMING SYSTEM ADMINISTERS THE COUP-DE-GRÂCE...

THE INTERNAL CRISES OF THE YANKEE EMPIRE, THE STRUGGLE FOR SOCIALISM IN VIETNAM, CUBA, CHILE, AFRICA, THE SPLITS INSIDE THE CHURCH, EVERY LIBERATION MOVEMENT... ARE ALL SIGNS OF CAPITALISM'S LAST STRUGGLES TO AVOID BEING WIPED OFF THE FACE OF THE EARTH...

Vietnam and Chile prove glaringly who the real enemy of humanity is...

Yeah! Greed!!

$$$$$

CAPITALISM HAS PROVEN ITSELF <u>UNABLE</u> TO SOLVE THE PROBLEMS OF THE PEOPLE LIVING UNDER IT (NOT TO MENTION PROBLEMS IN GENERAL OF HUMANITY) ... AND IT'S WELL ON THE ROAD TO FINAL CRISIS AND EVENTUAL COLLAPSE.

(Just as Charlie Marx "prophesized" it a century ago...)

THE PURPOSE OF MARX'S THEORY OF

HISTORICAL MATERIALISM

IS TO SHOW US THAT HISTORY IS <u>MADE</u> BY MAN, NOT BY "DESTINY" OR THE SO CALLED "HAND OF GOD"...

History is the life of people — period — that's all.

HUMANITY – THOUGHT MARX – DID NOT REQUIRE 'OUTSIDE' HELP TO INVENT ITS TOOLS. NO ANGEL APPEARED FROM HEAVEN TO TEACH MAN HOW TO CONSTRUCT PLOUGHS AND WHEELS...

Wheel ?!??
What I want to invent is the Lifebuoy!!

EACH GENERATION COMES ALONG TO CREATE, AND GRADUALLY PERFECT NEW TOOLS – BY WORKING AND NOT THANKS TO THE HOLY SPIRIT! (EVEN IF NOT ALL THE GREAT INVENTORS WERE ATHEISTS...)

BUT TOOLS CANNOT WORK ALL BY THEMSELVES.

PEOPLE HAVE TO SWEAT TO KEEP THEM OPERATING...

THESE INSTRUMENTS OF PRODUCTION, AND THE MEN WHO PRODUCE THINGS WITH THEM, ARE WHAT MARX CALLS...

The moving forces of society

BUT NOTHING IS PRODUCED IN ISOLATION. HUMAN LABOUR ALWAYS HAS
A SOCIAL CHARACTER. SOCIETY WAS FORMED BY MEN AS A HELP, AS A
PROTECTION AGAINST WILD ANIMALS, TO GET BETTER RESULTS FROM WORK...

(and to pull the wool over
our eyes...)

EXACTLY.
BECAUSE THIS IS WHAT EVENTUALLY
HAPPENED. THE OWNERS JOINED FORCES
TO SQUEEZE PRODUCTIVITY OUT OF THE
NON-OWNERS (I.E. THOSE WHO HAD
NOTHING BUT THEIR LABOUR-POWER...)

The work-force,
maestro...

(AND THAT'S HOW, AS WE'VE SEEN, THE
LEVELS OF SOCIAL CLASS AROSE, AND HOW
THE PRECISE KINDS OF RELATIONS
BETWEEN THEM WERE SET UP.
ONE EXPLOITERS,
THE OTHER EXPLOITED...)

THESE RELATIONS,
WHICH PEOPLE ESTABLISH
(LIKE 'EM OR NOT) DURING
THE PROCESS OF PRODUCTION,
MARX CALLS:

The relations
of production

THE COMBINATION OF "PRODUCTIVE FORCES" (OR UNITS OF PRODUCTION) AND THE RELATIONS OF PRODUCTION, MARX DEFINES BY THE CONCEPT OF

MODE OF PRODUCTION

Indeed, Marx says — History becomes the history of the modes of production...

HISTORY ISN'T JUST THE LIFE AND ADVENTURES OF NOBLES, KINGS, PRIESTS AND SUCH, BUT IT REVEALS THE SUCCESSIVE STAGES OF THE DIFFERENT MODES OF PRODUCTION BY WHICH MANKIND GAINED POWER OVER NATURE.

MARX DISTINGUISHES 5 SYSTEMS OR MODES THUS:

PRIMITIVE COMMUNITY

SLAVE STATE

FEUDAL STATE

CAPITALIST SYSTEM

SOCIALIST SOCIETY

127

PRIMITIVE COMMUNITY...

... AND THE SLAVE STATE ARE KNOWN AND CLEAR TO EVERYONE...

THE SYSTEM WE'LL NOW TRY TO EXPLAIN IS...

Feudalism (hoping everybody'll understand it!)

Now then my lad, What's this 'Feudalism' then?

FEUDALISM COMES FROM THE LATIN WORD, "FEUDUM", THE NAME GIVEN TO THE LANDS WHICH THE KING DIVIDED UP AMONG HIS NOBLES IN EXCHANGE FOR THEIR SUPPORT... (A "FEUDUM" = A "FEE")

THOSE WHO ACTUALLY LIVED ON THE LAND HAD SOME CLAIM TO THEIR BIT OF EARTH. BUT THEIR LABOUR BELONGED TO THE FEUDAL OVER-LORD TO WHOM THEY PAID TAXES AND WHO USED THEM WHENEVER HE WENT TO WAR... WHEN I SAY "KING" BY THE WAY, YOU CAN JUST AS WELL READ "POPE", BECAUSE THE CHURCH OF CHRIST WAS ALSO A FEUDAL SYSTEM LIKE ANY OTHER (AND PROBABLY WORSE...)

WITHIN FEUDALISM, THE SOCIAL CLASSES SEEN FROM TOP TO BOTTOM WERE:

NOBILITY

CLERGY

MERCHANT

GUILD ARTISANS

SERFS

AS TIME WENT ON, THE MERCHANTS AND GUILD
ARTISANS GREW IN NUMBERS AND POWER.
THEY BEGAN TO SHRUG OFF THE BURDENSOME
YOKE IMPOSED ON THEM BY THE NOBLES AND
CLERGY. THE FIRST INTELLECTUALS AWOKE,
BRINGING NEW IDEAS INTO DAYLIGHT.
A NEW CLASS IS BORN, THE

BOURGEOISIE

I'm really fed up with paying taxes to those lay-about
bishops and kings. Long live Liberty,
Damn it !!!

COMMERCE THUS BEGAN
TO CHANGE THE FORM OF
PRODUCTION.
THE BOURGEOISIE NEEDED
BIGGER (AND FREE) MARKETS
TO SHIFT THE MERCHANDISE
PRODUCED IN THEIR
WORKSHOPS. THEIR APPETITE
FOR PROFITS RAN SMACK
AGAINST THE LIMITS OF
THE FEUDAL MODE OF
PRODUCTION...
AND THESE RESTRAINTS
PROVOKED A SERIES OF
BOURGEOIS

REVOLUTIONS

AGAINST KINGS AND CHURCH,
LEADING TO THE BIRTH OF A
NEW "SYSTEM OF PRODUCTION":

CAPITALISM..

CAPITALISM IS ALREADY IN ITS VENERABLE OLD AGE. IN PRACTICE, IT SAW THE LIGHT OF DAY IN PARIS, 1789, WITH THE FRENCH REVOLUTION...

THE FRENCH REVOLUTION WAS PRIMARILY A LIBERATION MOVEMENT.
'LIBERATION' FROM WHAT?
FROM THE POWER OF THE MONARCH AND THE CLERGY.
FOR WHAT?
TO DEFEND PRIVATE PROPERTY AND FREE ENTERPRISE.
FOR WHOSE BENEFIT?
THE BOURGEOISIE, I.E. THE RICH WHO WANTED THE LIBERTY TO MAKE MORE MONEY AND THE LIBERTY OF THE SERFS SO AS TO BUY THEIR LABOUR FREELY.

THE FRENCH REVOLUTION WAS A GENERAL CLASS STRUGGLE, A TOUGH PITCHED BATTLE IN WHICH EVERYONE TOOK SIDES AGAINST THE COMMON ENEMY:
THE NOBILITY AND THE CLERGY.

ONCE DEFEATED, THEIR POWER WENT TO THE ASCENDING CLASS — THE BOURGEOISIE.
THE PEASANTRY GOT SOMETHING OUT OF IT: OWNERSHIP OF THEIR LANDS. BUT THE SERF-LABOURERS GOT NOTHING AT ALL...

Except the "liberty" to exchange masters...

THE BOURGEOIS REVOLUTION
(OR THE FRENCH: SAME DIFFERENCE)
WAS FOLLOWED BY ANOTHER
REVOLUTION — THE INDUSTRIAL.
HUMANITY INVENTED MACHINES
WHICH TOOK THE PLACE OF
MANUAL CRAFTS. THIS
COMPLETELY REVOLUTIONIZED
THE MODE OF PRODUCTION...

Oh sure!
But these 'effin'
machines won't
work 'emselves!!

THE APPEARANCE ON THE SCENE OF MACHINE-PRODUCED GOODS BRINGS
WITH IT A COUPLE OF NEW SOCIAL CLASSES: CAPITALISTS, OR
OWNERS, OF THE MACHINES, AND WORKERS, OR THE OPERATORS
TIED TO THESE INFERNAL MACHINES. WITH MACHINERY
COMES A NEW MODE OF PRODUCTION WHICH MARX
CALLS

CAPITALISM

NOW THE WORKER ISN'T THE
SLAVE OF A FEUDAL LORD.
HE'S A "FREE CITIZEN"
(I.E. FREE TO SELL
HIMSELF TO THE
"HIGHEST" BIDDER...)

Right! Anyone feel
like paying me more...?

JUST AS EVERYONE WAS SETTLING DOWN HAPPILY WITH CAPITALISM (AND *LIKE HEGEL*) THINKING THAT SOCIETY HAD FINALLY TAKEN THE RIGHT ROAD, ALONG COMES MARX AND SPOILS THE PARTY...

'Ere! Who the 'ell invited yon hippie??

MARX'S THEORY OF CLASS STRUGGLE—INEVITABLE AND HISTORICAL—REALLY HIT CAPITALISM BELOW THE BELT. SOONER OR LATER, SAYS MARX, CAPITALISM IS GOING TO HAVE TO RETREAT BEFORE A NEWER AND FAIRER SYSTEM...

Socialism

GULP!

MARX SHOWS US HOW THE LAWS OF HISTORICAL DEVELOPMENT <u>DETERMINE</u> THE INEVITABLE SEQUENCE OF MODES OF PRODUCTION: FROM PRIMITIVE TO SLAVERY, FROM FEUDALISM ON TO CAPITALISM... WHICH LED (AND STILL LEADS) MANY TO ASK THEMSELVES:

Then <u>why</u> the class struggle?

Why struggle for socialism, and fight the police, if it will happen anyway?

MARX Replies:

BECAUSE MEN MAKE HISTORY, NOT THE OTHER WAY ROUND...

HISTORY DOESN'T <u>DO</u> ANYTHING. IT DOESN'T PROMOTE ANY STRUGGLE.

CAPITAL WILL ATTEMPT TO RESIST ITS OWN DOWNFALL. WHAT WILL LEAD TO ITS DESTRUCTION ARE CAPITALISM'S INTERNAL CONTRADICTIONS: BUT ONLY BECAUSE OF AN ADVERSARY DEVELOPING INDEPENDENTLY OF CAPITALISM'S WILL, I.E. THE PROLETARIAT...

Only rain, hail and stuff like that fall from heaven. Change doesn't come from "on high"...

MARX KNOWS PERFECTLY WELL THAT THE RICH WILL NEVER <u>FREELY</u> SURRENDER THEIR WEALTH AND PRIVILEGES...

You gotta persuade 'em with "good manners!"

My word! I'd like to know how the plebeian riff-raff will take over...

HOW?

WELL, IF ANYONE REALLY WANTED TO KNOW (INCLUDING THIS FAT RUSSIAN FAUNTLEROY), MARX WILLINGLY EXPLAINED THE RECIPE FOR TRANSFORMING CAPITALIST SOCIETY INTO A SOCIALIST ONE: EXPROPRIATING THE PRIVATE MEANS OF PRODUCTION, REPLACING THE GOVERNMENT AND STATE ADMINISTRATION...
I.E. <u>SEIZING</u> POWER...

BUT HOW CAN THE WORKERS SEIZE POWER??

MARX SUPPLIES THE FORMULA IN THE COMMUNIST MANIFESTO...

WORKERS OF THE WORLD, UNITE!

A HAND IS MADE UP OF 5 FINGERS, BUT A FIST IS THE SAME 5 FINGERS UNITED...

(NOT FOR NOTHING, THE FIST IS THE SYMBOL OF THE WORKERS' STRUGGLE...)

AND SO?

MARX MAKES THE POINT CRYSTAL CLEAR — AS IN THIS ILLUSTRATION:

=

=

| A UNION | SEVERAL UNIONS | CONFEDERATION OF UNIONS |

"IN ITS STRUGGLE AGAINST THE UNITED POWER OF THE RULING CLASS, ONLY THE WORKING CLASS — AS AN ORGANISED CLASS — CAN ACTIVATE A PARTY OF ITS OWN TO OPPOSE ALL OTHER OLD, REACTIONARY PARTIES..."

THE FIRST STEP MUST BE TO CONVINCE THE WORKER THAT ONLY UNITY WILL GIVE HIM THE MEANS TO CHANGE HIS EXISTENCE. HE MUST BECOME AWARE OF HIS POWER, OF THE REASONS WHY HE LIVES BADLY, AND THAT CAPITALISM WILL NEVER SOLVE HIS PROBLEMS. HE MUST REALISE WHAT SOCIALISM CAN OFFER HIM...

... IN A WORD (HE'S GOT TO BE)

POLITICIZED

ONLY A POLITICIZED WORKING CLASS CAN MOVE TO THE NEXT STAGE: THE ORGANIZED STRUGGLE TO SAFEGUARD ITS RIGHTS...

EVEN IN MARX'S DAY, SOME ALREADY BELIEVED THAT UNION CAMPAIGNS ONLY SERVED TO OBTAIN HIGHER WAGES AND BETTER LIVING CONDITIONS... BUT, SAYS MARX, THIS IS THE WRONG WAY TO UNDERSTAND UNIONS...

"Communists fight for the attainment of the immediate aims, for the enforcement of the momentary interests of the working class, but in the movement of the present, they also represent and take care of the future of that movement"...

(Manifesto)

THE PRINCIPLE AIM OF ANY LABOUR UNION MUST BE CHANGE WHICH ANTICIPATES SOCIALISM ... OR ELSE IT JUST WASTES ITS TIME, AS AMERICAN UNIONS DO, STRUGGLING ALONG ON BENDED KNEE FOR CAPITALISM'S SAKE ...

THANKS BOSS!
FOR THE LOVELY RAISE

NOW COMES THE INTERESTING QUESTION, WHICH MANY READERS HAVE PROBABLY ASKED THEMSELVES: PEACEFUL ROAD OR ARMED STRUGGLE? WHICH?

Ranged against the working-man's party, there's the U.S. government... the army, the police, laws, repression, the whole propaganda machine!

... and I'll add a dash of what's missing— like in Chile!..

CIA

SOONER OR LATER — MARX SAID — THE CONFRONTATION HAS GOT TO TURN DEADLY, AND THE WORKING CLASS WILL ARRIVE AT REVOLUTION. A WORKERS' PARTY MAY HELP THE PROLETARIAT TO SCREW CONCESSIONS FROM THE CAPITALISTS, BUT EVEN THAT WON'T CHANGE THE BASIC EXPLOITIVE CONDITIONS (MORE OR LESS EXPLOITED, MAYBE, BUT NEVER COMPLETELY FREE ...)

THE STRUGGLE OF
INDUSTRIAL AND
AGRARIAN WORKERS
WITHIN THE FRAME
OF UNIONS, PARTIES
AND EVEN PARLIAMENT,
IS ONLY A WAY TO
PREPARE, TO ORGANIZE,
TO GAIN THE STRENGTH
FOR THE DECISIVE BLOW...

"... in times when the class struggle nears the decisive hour, the process of dissolution going on within the ruling class, in fact within the whole range of old society, assumes such a violent, glaring character..."

"... that a small section of the ruling class cuts itself adrift, and joins the revolutionary class... just as, at an earlier period, a section of the nobility went over to the bourgeoisie..." *(Manifesto)*

THIS "SMALL SECTION" CUTTING ITSELF ADRIFT FROM THE BOURGEOISIE INCLUDES INTELLECTUALS, LIKE MARX AND ENGELS, LENIN, MAO, HO CHI MINH, FIDEL CASTRO, CHE, AND LOTS OF OTHERS WHO WOULD HAVE DONE NOTHING ALONE... LIKE THE STUDENTS WHO WON'T CHANGE ANYTHING UNLESS THEY JOIN FORCES WITH THE WORKERS AND PEASANTS...

140

(amen!!)

MARX NEVER IMAGINED A WORKING CLASS MOVEMENT SEPARATE FROM SOCIALIST THEORY. A SOCIALIST PARTY WITHOUT MASS SUPPORT IS A PHANTOM, A BODY WITHOUT A HEAD, OR VICE VERSA, LIKE THE LEFTIST PARTIES WHICH HAVE LOST TOUCH WITH THE REAL PROBLEMS OF WORKERS AND PEASANTS...

MARX'S THEORY HAD TO WAIT 24 YEARS AFTER HIS DEATH BEFORE BEING PUT INTO PRACTICE, AND IN A COUNTRY WHERE IT SEEMED IMPOSSIBLE. IN RUSSIA, 1917, THANKS TO THE VISION AND STEADFAST STRUGGLE OF A "BOURGEOIS" MARXIST CALLED

..."THE TEACHING OF MARX IS ALL-POWERFUL BECAUSE IT IS TRUE. IT IS COMPLETE AND HARMONIOUS, PROVIDING MEN WITH A CONSISTENT VIEW OF THE UNIVERSE, WHICH CANNOT BE RECONCILED WITH ANY SUPERSTITION, ANY REACTION, ANY DEFENCE OF BOURGEOIS OPPRESSION. IT IS THE LAWFUL SUCCESSOR OF THE BEST THAT HAS BEEN CREATED BY HUMANITY IN THE 19th CENTURY — GERMAN PHILOSOPHY, ENGLISH POLITICAL ECONOMY AND FRENCH SOCIALISM."

("The 3 Sources and 3 Component Parts of Marxism" 1913 V.19)

LENIN WAS THE ONE TO CONTINUE MARX'S IDEAS. HE CONTRIBUTED GREATLY TO REVOLUTIONARY THEORY, DEFENDING IT AGAINST ITS ENEMIES AND MISTAKEN INTERPRETERS. HE WAS THE ONE TO PROVE MARX CORRECT...

But Marx, basing himself on the experience of the Paris Commune, taught that the proletariat *cannot* simply lay hold of the ready-made state machine and use it for its own purposes, that the proletariat must *smash* this machine and substitute a new one for it... This new type of state machinery was created by the Paris Commune, and by the Russian Soviets of Workers...

(Lenin, Vol.26, p.90)

(BUT TO GO ON ABOUT LENIN AND THE RUSSIAN REVOLUTION CALLS FOR A WHOLE OTHER BOOK...)

... I THINK THIS IS THE RIGHT PLACE TO WRITE

The End...

(... well, not entirely...)

A LITTLE DICTIONARY
OF MARXIST TERMS...*

* You're not obliged to read this now! Declare a holiday and start again — later on!
And I hope it will be clearer than the preceding pages...

AGNOSTICISM / (from the Greek, *agnostos* = unknown). Philosophical doctrine which maintains that human reason is limited and the true nature of things inaccessible to man. This doctrine holds that the world we observe and deal with is not an objective reality, but rather a product of the activity of our reason and sense organs. Agnosticism is disproved by experience and practice, now that science has cleared the way to the knowledge of things. There remains one difference: between what is already known and what is not yet known.

Agnostic philosophers include Hume, Kant, Comte, Spencer, Mach etc.

ANALYSIS and SYNTHESIS / 1) analysis (in Greek, 'decomposition'), dis-integration of an object or phenomenon into its simple component parts. 2) synthesis (in Greek, 'composition'), recombination of the parts of an object or phenomenon as a whole.

Metaphysics opposes analysis to synthesis. Dialectical materialism, instead, maintains the unity of these two procedures. "Without analysis there is no synthesis" (Engels). For example, when analysing the human body, anatomists study its organs separately; but to grasp the complete, deep significance and function of every organ, analysis is not enough. It is necessary to consider the organism as a whole: indeed, studying its parts, but as a synthesis.

ANIMISM / (from the Latin, *anima*: soul). The spiritualization of natural phenomena. The belief that behind every natural object there hides an invisible or 'mental' spirit-force. "This tendency to personification had as a consequence the creation of the gods." (Engels). Primitive animism was the basis of religion and later idealist thought.

ANTAGONISM / (from the Greek, *agon* = contest). An irreconcilable contradiction which is resolved by violence. As the contradiction between the bourgeoisie and the working class is thus resolved by socialist revolution. Contradictions between the working class and peasantry have no antagonistic character.

ATHEISM / (from the Greek, 'without god') The scientific negation of religion. Atheism was born in ancient Greece with the materialist philosophers, Democritus and Epicurus, who denied the supernatural and stated that the world is nothing other than matter composed of atoms.

ANTI-DUHRING / The abbreviated title of a work by Engels: "The Scientific Revolution of Eugene Duhring", a classic of Marxist literature. The work was aimed against the German philosopher, Duhring, who wished to refute Marxism by recourse to metaphysics. The ANTI-DUHRING is a masterly synthesis of Marx's forty years of struggle and study.

ATOM / The idea of the atom was first introduced to science by Democritus and Epicurus, more than 2,000 years ago. The physicist, Newton, and the philosophers, Holbach and Gassendi, worked on this theory.

BASE (or INFRA) and SUPERSTRUCT-URE/ The mode of production, i.e. the forces and relations of production which constitute the economic base - the foundation of society. Once the base (or infra-structure) is modified then the super-structure (including the political system, religion, philosophy, morality, art, science etc.) must also modify itself, at a more or less rapid rhythm. (see also ECONOMIC BASE)

CAPITAL / or 'Das Kapital', the principal work by Karl Marx. A detailed analysis of the laws governing the economic development of capitalism — but also an immense historical and philosophical treatise. In this work, the theory of historical materialism is fundamentally developed.

CATEGORIES / Notions which express the essential relations and laws of the real world. In dialectical materialism, these categories are: matter, motion, space, time, necessity, causality, quantity, substance, form, content, etc. In Historical Materialism, they are: the social-economic structure, forces of production, infra-and super-structure, ideology, etc.

These categories represent a generalization of the processes and phenomena of nature, independent of the consciousness of man.

CAUSALITY / One of the forms of general interdependence of phenomena in the objective world. In essence, cause and effect "are only moments of interdependence and universal relation, of the connection of events; they are, above all, present in the chain of the development of matter." (Lenin) There can be no phenomena (events) without causes. All natural phenomena have natural and material causes. Cause and effect stand in reciprocal relation to each other. Between them exists an internal relation regulated by laws.

Thus in the socialist system, the development of technology becomes a *cause* of the increasing well-being (*effect*) of workers.

CLASS STRUGGLE (see also **SOCIAL CLASSES**) / Struggle between exploited and exploiters. Demonstration that class interests are irreconcilable. The forms of class struggle are diverse: economic, political, ideological, theoretical. But all such kinds are subordinate to the *political* struggle. With the establishment of the dictatorship of the proletariat, class struggle does not cease but takes on new forms.

COMMUNISM / The doctrine of Marx and Engels founded on the basis of the materialist conception of history. Communism is the stage following after socialism and when social classes cease to exist. Communism does not yet exist in any country. The Soviet Union, China and other socialist countries are still in the phase of socialism where class struggle has still not terminated.

CONDITIONS OF THE MATERIAL LIFE OF SOCIETY / The elements determining the conditions of material life in society are: 1) geographical situation and natural resources; 2) population density; 3) the mode of production by which it creates the material goods necessary to its existence.

The fundamental force which determines development of a society, and also its passage from one kind of social system to another, is material production — the development of the "productive power of the society".

DARWIN, CHARLES (1809-1882) / Celebrated English thinker, founder of the theory of evolution. "Darwin put an end to the belief that the animal and vegetable species bear no relation to one another, except by chance, and that they were created by God, and hence immutable." (Lenin)

DETERMINISM and **INDETERMINISM** / *Determinism*: doctrine concerning the necessary relationship between events and phenomena and their accidental conditioning. For example, the anarchy of the capitalist mode of production fatally *determines* economic crisis; the development of class struggle inevitably *determines* a social revolution.

Idealists oppose to determinism, *indeterminism* — maintaining that the natural course of events in reality are not subject to laws but to independent, arbitrary chance.

DIALECTIC / (from the Greek, 'debate' and 'converse') According to early Greek philosophers, the art of knowing truth by uncovering the contradictions in the reasonings of one's adversary. Later, dialectics (also sometimes in the form, 'dialectic') came to be transformed into a theory of development and universal relations. Dialectics considers all phenomena as being in movement, in process of perpetual change. It views the development of nature itself as a result of the struggle between contradictions within nature. Dialectics became a science when Marx and Engels liberated it from Hegelian idealism. It is a doctrine of development — a science of the universal laws governing the development of nature, human society and thought.

DICTATORSHIP OF THE PROLETARIAT / The period of transition from socialism to communism, during which the material conditions are created for socialist construction, the suppression of classes and the passage to a classless and stateless society.

DOGMA, DOGMATISM / Dogma is undemonstrated affirmation, accepted with blind faith. This is why Marx and Engels always said: "Our doctrine is not a dogma, but a guide to action." Unfortunately, dogmatic Marxists often ignore this crucial aspect of Marxism, and thereby rob it of its revolutionary, creative power.

DUALISM / (from the Latin, 'two') A philosophical tendency opposed to 'monism' (from the Greek, *monos* = one, unity). Dualism places not one but two different substances at the origin of existence. Thus DESCARTES sees man as being composed of two distinct substances: one, material — the body, the other spiritual — the soul. Marxism places matter-in-movement at the origin of all natural phenomena as primary cause. Consciousness is a secondary cause produced by matter.

ECLECTICISM / Mere mechanical link-ups of various currents, concepts and theories, without any pre-established principle. Eclectic thinkers attempt to reconcile materialism and idealism.

ECONOMIC BASE / The mode of production at the basis of any social system. The economic base (or infra-structure) determines the totality of the social super-structure: the state, political institutions, ideas and theories, etc. "The structures of every society can change rapidly only by revolutionizing the economic base." (Marx)

ECONOMIC STRUCTURE / Ordering of society into classes: the *relations* of production which correspond to the specific level determined by the development of the *material* forces of production.

EMPIRIO-CRITICISM / Reactionary, idealist current of philosophy which arose in Germany and Austria during the second half of the 19th century. Its initiators were Avenarius and Mach. They affirmed that "elements of the world" i.e. "elements of experience" stood at the basis of all phenomena. Each thing is a "combination of elements". By the term 'elements', they meant the fact that sensation is at the basis of phenomena; but in such a way as to identify 'element' with sense-impression.

EPICURUS / (342-270 B.C.) Greek materialist philosopher, teacher and follower of Democritus.

EVOLUTION and **REVOLUTION** / Quantitative changes, of an unperceived, slow and interrupted kind come about through evolution. Qualitative changes, on the contrary, happen all at once, by leaps, in a revolutionary manner. Development implies both, necessarily. Evolution prepares the way for revolution. But opportunism replaces revolutionary struggle by reform.

EXISTENCE Philosophic term designating *subjective* reality, in matter.

EXISTENCE and **SOCIAL CONSCIOUS-NESS** / From the viewpoint of dialectical materialism, existence is primary while consciousness, as a simple reflection of matter, of nature, of human thought, is secondary. Social existence — i.e. the mode of producing material goods, objects, food, clothing etc. — is the primary element which determines social consciousness and the spiritual, intellectual life of society (its culture). Marx extended materialism into the areas of social phenomena by discovering that social existence and the mode of production determine social consciousness.

EXPERIMENT / By experiment is currently understood the 'practical experience' of the procedures verifying knowledge by direct observation of phenomena — either in the laboratory or in objective reality.
Philosophy explains *experiment* either in materialist or idealist form. For dialectical materialism, experience presupposes the presence of an objective, material world which exists independently of human consciousness. But for idealism, experience does not involve material objects or even phenomena: rather, it is concerned with our past impressions. It can therefore consider religious 'sentiment' alone as *experimental* proof enough of the existence of God.

FATALISM / (from the Latin, 'fate') Idealist notion which holds that historical development is pre-determined by some unknown force, by 'destiny'. Fatalism denies the *creative* function of people, history and political struggle, and considers humanity a plaything in the hands of God or fate, unable to influence things through ACTION.

FETISHISM / To deify or 'fetishize' objects means to give them occult, supernatural forces foreign to human nature. In primitive times, the fetish was an object of awe; later becoming a good or bad luck charm. In capitalism, the fetishism of money, property and commodities is the magic of capitalist ownership.

FEUERBACH, LUDWIG (1804-72) / One of the major German materialists who proclaimed and defended atheism and influenced the founders of Marxism. Feuerbach, however, remains idealist in his concept of social phenomena. Neglecting the material basis of society, he distinguished the successive stages of human development according to the different forms of religious consciousness. Feuerbach did not grasp the importance of practical revolutionary action, or the dialectical interaction between man and nature and the transformation of humanity in the process of production.

FIDE-ISM / (from the Latin, *fides*: 'faith') Doctrine (especially in Latin countries) which replaces understanding by faith and stresses the determining role it plays. Lenin sees idealist philosophy as a "more or less weakened or diluted fide-ism"; so to speak, a clericalism. (see IDEALISM)

FORCES OF PRODUCTION / Instruments or tools with which material goods are produced; also *persons* who use these productive tools and manufacture material goods, thanks to experience and work-training. Productive forces (machines, tools, raw materials etc.) and human labour-power must be present as the indispensable elements of work. Social life depends upon productive forces which it can command and the modes of production employed. Hence the importance of the *social planning* of these forces, which will only bear fruit with socialism.

FORM and **CONTENT** / In nature, society or thought, everything has its content and form. Agrarian reform, for instance, may be the content; but its form may vary according to the modes of application.

FORMAL LOGIC / Theory concerning the laws of human thought which separates nature from the enquiry into those laws. Formal logic does not preoccupy itself with material truth (i.e. the faithful reflection and conception of natural phenomena), but with 'formal' truth. Hence its name. Herein lies the basis of metaphysical method. Dialectics (i.e. natural logic) is the contrary of formal logic since it considers that the content of thought, the principles and laws of logic, must correspond to materiality, nature and its regulative laws. Formal logic affirms that all objects and concepts are equal to themselves (i.e. the concept of *formal* identity: that A=A). Dialectical materialism shows that every object *is* and *is not* self-identical because it is caught up in a process of development.

FREEDOM and **NECESSITY** / Metaphysicians often contrast freedom to necessity. Some affirm that will is absolutely free, i.e. unconditioned. Others hold that free will does not exist, but only absolute necessity. Either freedom or necessity . . . From the Marxist viewpoint, these positions are un-scientific, because freedom does not merely consist of imaginary independence vis-a-vis the laws of nature, but of knowledge of these laws and the possibility of applying them positively in practical action. "Freedom", Engels says, "consists of a domination over self and external nature; a domination based on the knowledge of the necessities of nature. Consequently, freedom is *conscious necessity*. Without an understanding of necessity, real liberty is unattainable."

HEGEL, GEORG WILHELM FRIEDRICH / (1770-1831) German philosopher, idealist dialectician. Nature, according to Hegel, does not develop across time, but varies eternally only in space. The most valuable part of idealist Hegelian philosophy is the dialectical method it employs — that ideas develop from dialectical contradictions; that transformations from quantity to quality have their origin in this development; that truth is concrete; that the developmental process of human society is realized by its submission to laws and not by chance or under the pressure of outsized personalities. Yet, Hegel was pusillanimous and inconsistent: he bowed before the Prussian feudal monarchy, and minimized the extremes of his dialectical positions out of fear and self-interest. "My dialectical method," Marx said, "is not only distinct from Hegelian method at bottom, but is absolutely opposed to it." For Hegel, thought creates reality. The opposite for Marx — ideas are nothing more than matter absorbed and transformed by human thought.

HUMANISM / Cultural current, developed from the 14th to the 16th centuries.

Conception of social reality proper to the then new-born bourgeoisie which struggled to liberate human personality and science from bondage to religious feudalism. Petrarch, Boccaccio, Erasmus, Machiavelli etc., were some representatives of bourgeois humanism. Humanism cannot survive under a capitalist regime because it is opposed to the exploitation of man by man, the very essence of capitalism. Only the real liberation of humanity can bring about genuine humanism.

HUME, DAVID / (1711-1776) English bourgeois philosopher, historian and economist. As an agnostic, he reckoned insoluble the problem of the existence or non-existence of objective reality. He affirmed that we cannot know what things are in themselves and whether they exist or not. Denying the material basis of things and causality, Hume concluded that what alone exists is a flux of psychological perception in human consciousness, and that science leads only to the simple description of this current, with little possibility either of understanding or of conceiving its laws.

IDEALISM / Philosophy which considers reality as an incarnation of a 'universal Idea' or of a 'consciousness'. Idealism is closely linked with religion and leads more or less openly to the idea of God.

IDEOLOGY / Combination of ideas, assumptions, notions of determined concepts, representations. Politics, science, morality, art and religion are *forms* of ideology. All ideologies are reflections of social existence. In class-based society, ideology expresses and defends the interests of the classes in struggle. In bourgeois society, struggle develops between bourgeois and socialist ideologies. There is no intermediate term, since, as Lenin affirms, humanity has not elaborated a 'third' ideology.

INDUCTION (and **DEDUCTION**) / *Induction:* method of reasoning which consists of passing from the particular to the general, from facts to generalizations. *Deduction:* method which consists of passing from the general to the particular, from generalized propositions to particular conclusions.

INSTRUMENTS (or **TOOLS**) **OF PRO-RODUCTION** / Principle elements of productive forces (e.g. machinery) employed by humanity to act upon nature and transform it into material goods. Marx says that economic epochs differ from each other not so much in what they produce but *how* they do so. How labour produces. The means of production are not simply measures of human labour-power but also the indication of the *relations* by means of which work takes place.

KANT, IMMANUEL / (1724-1804) Founder of classical German idealism. He attempted to reconcile materialism and idealism. "When Kant admits that a certain 'thing-in-itself', outside us, must correspond to our representation of it, then he is a materialist. When he declares it impossible to know this 'thing-in-itself', he becomes an idealist." (Lenin) As Kant himself declares, the central problem of his theory of knowledge is to define the limits of the laws of reason, while still retaining a place for God beyond such limits. In his doctrine of ethics, Kant believes it 'necessary' to recognize the existence of God and the soul's immortality, so as to maintain a basis for morality.

MARXISM-LENINISM / Theory of the proletarian liberation movement. Theory and practice of the dictatorship of the proletariat. Theory of the construction of communist society.

MATTER / (or **MATERIAL**) By its nature, the world is material. The variety of phenomena in nature corresponds to the distinct forms of *matter in motion.* Lenin wrote that matter is a philosophical category to designate objective reality which presents itself to humanity through human perception. Matter is copied, 'photographed' or reflected through human sensations while retaining an existence proper to itself and independent of them.

MATERIALISM / One of the two main tendencies in philosophy which gives a specific reply to the fundamental problem of the relation between thought and existence. Materialism recognizes matter as the primary element, and consciousness (or thought) secondary. It relies on science — particularly the physical sciences. Dialectical

materialism recuperates the entire materialist tradition preceding it and re-elaborates everything of value in it.
(see below)

MATERIALISM (DIALECTICAL) /
Philosophical doctrine formulated by Marx and Engels, so called because of its *dialectical* manner of confronting, studying and understanding natural phenomena; and *materialist* by its manner of interpreting phenomena and drawing up its theory. Dialectical materialism is the only scientific interpretation of the world; and it is opposed to idealism which offers an interpretation based on religion.

MATERIALISM (HISTORICAL) / Marxist
doctrine of the development of human society. Historical materialism sees in the development of material goods necessary to human existence the primary force which determines all social life (and which conditions the transition from one kind of social order to another).
The growth of human power over nature finds its expression in the development of the productive forces of society. The transmutation of economic-social forces throughout history (primitive communal, slave, feudal and capital states) is, above all, a change from certain kinds of productive *modes* and *relations* towards other more progressive ones. Such change is the necessary effect, the cause of which are the laws to which social productive forces everywhere submit.
Discovery of the real basis of life and social development (material production) allows one to see for the first time the importance of the creative spirit of the masses. Great men were not the ones *alone* to make history, but the workers, the real prime movers of the production process, those who accomplished the material tasks necessary for social subsistence.

MATERIALISM (MECHANISTIC) / Early
form of materialism which sought to explain all natural phenomena by mechanical laws. It considers motion not as *change* in general but as the mechanical displacement of bodies in space due to external influences — the mere collision of two entities. Mechanistic materialism denies the spontaneous movement of bodies, their qualitative change, the development by leaps, the passage from inferior to superior.

METAPHYSICS / (from the Greek, *ta meta
ta physika*: those works of Aristotle after his 'Physics') Metaphysical method affirms that things and their mental reflections (i.e. concepts) are essentially discrete, unchanging, petrified, given once for all, and can thus be investigated separately, independently one from the other. Metaphysics posits in principle that nature is at rest, immobile, unchanging and unmoving. It considers the process of development uniquely on a quantitative and not qualitative level. Politically, the stance is one that denies class struggle and tries to show that the transition from capitalism to socialism can be realized without violent rupture, by peaceful fusion of capitalism with socialism.

METHODOLOGY / Doctrine of method:
combination of procedures, techniques of enquiry applicable to all sciences.

MONISM / (from the Greek, *monos*: one)
Philosophical doctrine which, contrary to dualism, recognizes as the cause of all existence only a single principle or origin. Materialists, for instance, consider *matter* as the unique cause of all phenomena; and the idealist-monist, spirit or god or mind.

MORALITY, MORALS / Norms of social
life, human behaviour, one of the forms of social consciousness. Materialists hold that morality changes with each change of social order. There exists a morality typical of the slave state; another in the feudal state, the bourgeois, and the communist. The ruling class imposes 'its' morality and puts it into practice in accord with its historical class interests.

NEGATION OF NEGATION / The law of
the negation of negation is fundamental to dialectics. Every phenomenon, because internally contradictory, contains in itself its own proper negation (or its own opposite). Thus, within it unfolds the conflict between what *was* and what is *becoming* — between old and new. Negation of the past state is not, however, a pure or vain negation, a simple annulment of everything which has been (as metaphysics thinks.) "Negation, in dialectics, does not signify merely saying No, or simply saying

something does not exist, or destroying it in some manner." (Engels) Dialectics demands "demonstration of the relation between the negative and the positive: so as to encounter the positive in the negative." (Lenin) Communism, thus, declares that everything positive has been created by humanity — even what was obtained under the yoke of capitalism. This is the positive in the negative. Communist society, in its turn, is the negation of the exploitative class regime — i.e. the negation of the negation.

OBJECTIVE / Opposite of subjective: what exists outside human consciousness, independently, but which human thought genuinely reflects.

PANTHEISM / (from the Greek, *pan*: all, and *theos*: god) Philosophical doctrine according to which divinity, as a spiritual and impersonal first principle, is found throughout nature — so that everything is divine.

PLATO / (427-347 B.C.) Greek philosopher, ideologist of the slave-owning aristocracy; founder of objective idealism which maintains that there exists besides the universe of perceptible things *another* world — the one of Ideas. So, above and beyond the trees one actually sees (which derive from various essences), Plato affirms there exists *the* unique Idea one has of 'trees', which is always identical, eternal — and this is the case for all of nature. According to Plato, things are only the shadows of Ideas. Ideas are eternal; things transitory. Not perception, but reason and its concepts give one true knowledge of the essence of things in reality.

PHILOSOPHY / (from the Greek, *philos*: love, friend, and *sophia*: science or wisdom) In dialectical materialism, the science of the most general laws of nature, human society and thought. The fundamental problem of philosophy is that of the relation between existence and thought. To find the answer, all philosophical tendencies divide up into two camps — materialist and idealist.

PHILOSOPHY, THE CLASSICAL GERMAN / Of the 18th and first half of the 19th centuries. Kant, its founder, was succeeded by Fichte and Schelling. Hegel's system represents the culminating phase of this philosophical movement. Classical German philosophy reflects the influences of European revolutionary movements. But such influences were deflected by the retrogressive socio-economic conditions of the epoch. This philosophy did contribute something fundamental — the renewal of dialectics as the theory of development. Taken up by Marx, it served as the basis for dialectical materialism. Engels has brilliantly analysed this philosophy in his work, "Ludwig Feuerbach And The End Of Classical German Philosophy."

POSITIVISM / One of the most widespread of the idealist currents within modern bourgeois philosophy. Positivism, according to its founders, is based not upon abstract deductions but on 'positive', real facts. August Comte, its creator, believed that the human mind must renounce any effort to know the very essence of things and content itself with the truth derived from observation and experiment. But this is only an "up to date" agnosticism.

PROPERTY / Private property appeared long after the origins of humanity. In the primitive communal state, ownership of the means of production was held in common. In the slave state, the 'boss' was the owner of human means of production — and hence the origin of private property. Under socialism, the means of production belong to the community, not to particular individuals — hence *socialist* property.

RATIONALISM / Theory which tends to recognize reason as the unique source of true knowledge; contrary to *empiricism* which makes perception this source of knowledge. Descartes and Leibnitz were outstanding representatives of rationalism.

RELATIONS OF PRODUCTION / Reciprocal relations established between people in the process of producing material goods. Persons can produce goods, not only individually, but together by uniting and practising communal action. History determines five main types of such relations: 1) In the primitive communal state, ownership of the instruments of production and products was held in common. With the passage from stone tools to metal, the tribes turned to agriculture and commerce and began to accumulate commodities. This led to the birth of private property, and monopolizing of accumulated wealth by a minority, and the rise of classes — the owners and the slaves. 2) In the slave epoch, free labour was replaced by slave exploitation: land was parcelled out to his serfs who worked for him partly freely, partly by payment in kind. 4) With the rise of the bourgeois or pre-capitalist society, a minority capitalist class seizes the means of production and exploits a wage-earning class. 5) The socialist state restores common ownership of the means of production, gives the product back to the producer, and eliminates ruling class exploitation.

RELIGION / Combination of beliefs and cult-practices which subordinates human life to a divine super-order. It appears in history as a form of oppression of the people by the ruling class. Marxism sees in religion the exploitation of human ignorance and credulity.

REVISIONISM / Hostile counter-current to Marxism which seeks to 'correct' he philosophical foundations of dialectical materialism. Today, for instance, China and the USSR accuse each other of 'revisionism' in their modes of applying socialism.

SCHOLASTICISM / (from Latin, *schola*, school; and Greek *skhole*, leisure) Gathered under this name are the various schools of philosophy current in the Middle Ages. But each one was linked strictly to religious dogma, all equally "servants of theology", all overlooked reality. Such dogmatism lends its name, 'scholastic', to all reasoning foreign to reality, all groundless philosophies, certain political discussions, etc. The main scholastics (or school-men) were Thomas Aquinas, Anselm of Canterbury, Duns Scotus, William of Occam, etc.

SOCIALISM / Economy, social and political doctrine which expresses the struggle for the equal distribution of wealth by eliminating private property and the exploitative ruling class. In practice, such a distribution of wealth is achieved by *social* ownership of the means of production, exchange and diffusion.

SOCIALISM (UTOPIAN) / Non-scientific socialism based on imaginary or optimist theories. Upheld by certain French and English utopian-socialists of the 19th century.

SOCIOLOGY / Science of society; as founded by Comte and Herbert Spencer, it takes no account of class struggle. Marx succeeded in raising sociology to a science by demonstrating that the development of society is not solely determined by *ideas* but by the *relations* of production. Thus he showed the course of ideas obeys the course of things. Marx also made clear that the problem of scientific research into society consists of the explanation of those particular historical laws which regulate the origin, existence, development and decline of any given social organism, and its transformation into another, superior one.

SOPHISM, SOPHISTRY / Incorrect reasoning presented in such a way as to appear correct, or persuasive, and thus which leads others into error. Sophistry is the application in discussion of such erroneous conclusions. The characteristic method of sophistry is: "To start from external resemblances between facts, apart from their relation to events." (Lenin) By relying on apparent resemblances, sophists seek to apply the properties of one set of phenomena to others completely different.

SPINOZA, BARUCH / (1632-77) Jewish-Dutch philosopher, denied the existence of God as creator of nature. Considered that God was nature itself. By thus calling nature God, he explained that nature was its own cause. He continued the rationalism of Descartes, although his system was monist — a system in which thought originates in nature.

STATE / Political organization of the economically dominant class, having as its aim the defence of the existing economic order (status quo) — but also the annihilation of the resistance put up against it by other classes. "The state is a machine to maintain the domination of one class over another." (Lenin)

TIME AND SPACE / These represent the objective form of the existence of matter. Time and space are inseparable from matter, and vice-versa. Dialectical materialism teaches that nothing exists in the world outside of or beyond matter in motion, and that matter cannot move except in space and time. Opposing itself to materialism, idealism believes time and space to be products of human thought and it separates these categories from matter.

THEOLOGY / Pseudo-science which seeks to give foundation to religion by borrowing from philosophical argumentation.

THESIS, ANTITHESIS, SYNTHESIS / (from the Greek: affirmation, negation, union) Every process of development, according to Hegel passes through these three stages: thesis, anti-thesis, syn-thesis. Each stage refutes the one before, and the last re-unites in itself the dominant features of the first two — hence its name, 'synthesis'. This is the 'surface' aspect of dialectics.

UNITY AND CONFLICT BETWEEN CONTRARIES / Opposing metaphysics, dialectics posits on principle that internal contradictions belong properly to all objects and natural phenomena, and within them everything is continually in motion, ever-changing. Each thing represents in itself the unity of contraries. Everything has a past and a future, a development and a decline, a positive and a negative aspect. This is why movement from a lower to a higher state is achieved by the struggle between opposite tendencies. Within the capitalist mode of production, the proletariat and the bourge-oisie are at once related and opposed through struggle.

Recommended further reading

"We shall not end, but break off. You can continue these considerations, ladies and gentlemen, with – but even more profoundly without – the aid of any good bookshop." (Walter Benjamin, 'Radio Talk on Brecht', 1930)

Whether what the French philosopher J.P. Sartre said nearly forty years ago – that we cannot go beyond Marxism "because we have not gone beyond the circumstances which engendered it" – is true or not depends, to coin a phrase, on the circumstances. However, Marxism continues to be a focus of political, social, economic, cultural and even theological debate. The literature on Marx and Marxism is therefore vast. This list is a practical one which limits itself to Marx's own texts, all (except the *Collected Works*) available in paperback and a few subsidiary works. An * indicates a substantial bibliography.

Texts

The best way to study Marx is to read what he (often with Engels) wrote. His most famous short works – *The Communist Manifesto; The Eighteenth Brumaire of Louis Napoleon; The Civil War in France; The Critique of the Gotha Programme; Poverty of Philosophy; Preface and Introduction to 'A Contribution to a Critique of Political Economy'; Wages, Labour and Capital; Wages, Prices; Profit;* and a (very) *Selected Letters* – are available in pamphlet form published by Foreign Language Press, Beijing, generally only from specialist bookshops, as are his *Economic and Philosophic MS of 1844* (Lawrence and Wishart).

The best paperback edition of Marx is the nine-volume Penguin Classic edition, with one exception. This consists of four volumes by political and philosophical writings (*Early Writings*, ed. and intro. by Lucio Colletti; *The Revolutions of 1848; Surveys from Exile; The First International and After*, all 3 vols ed. and intro. by Lucio Colletti; *The Revolutions of 1848; Surveys from Exile; The First International and After*, all 3 vols ed. and intro. by David Fernbach); *Capital*, 3 vols, ed . and intro. by Ernest Mandel; the *Grundrisse*, ed. and introduced by Martin Nicolaus; and – the exception – an edition of the *Communist Manifesto* with a splenetically hostile introduction and feeble notes by A.J.P. Taylor. This is well replaced by the Norton Critical Edition of the *Manifesto* (ed. and intro. by Frederic L. Bender) which, like all the other Penguins, is soundly edited and stimulatingly introduced.

Other selections are *The Portable Karl Marx* (ed. Eugen Kamenka) in Penguin; *The Marx-Engels Reader* (ed. Robert Tucker) (Norton); and

*Readings from Karl Marx** (ed. Derek Sayer) (Routledge). Two useful 'Student editions' are *Capital* and *The German Ideology* (containing the famous *Theses on Feuerbach* (ed. C.J. Arthur) (Lawrence and Wishart). For those who want their Marx, and Engels, as complete as possible in English, the *Collected Works* is approaching completion (forty volumes out of the final fifty available so far). This edition is organized into four parts – Early Philosophical Works (vols 1-3), General Works in chronological order (vols 4-27), Economic Works (vols 28-37), and Letters (vols 38-50) (Lawrence and Wishart and International Publishers).

Commentaries

*The Cambridge Companion to Marx** (ed. Terrell Carver) (Cambridge University Press) contains essays on reception history, philosophy, aesthetics, feminism, and gender politics. Tom Bottomore's *A Dictionary of Marxist Thought** (Blackwell) is a comprehensive dictionary of Marxism and its terminology.

The most thorough critical history and assessment of Marx and Marxism is Leszek Kolakowski's *Main Currents of Marxist Thought** (Oxford University Press, 3 vols), including Engels, Bernstein, Kautsky, Lenin, Luxemburg, Trotsky, Gramsci, Mao, Lukacs, and the Frankfurt School; in contrast, the briefest, limiting itself to Marx, is Peter Singer's Past Master *Marx* (also OUP).

Biographies

The most comprehensive is David McLellan's *Karl Marx – His Life and Thought** (Macmillan); the most attractive to read is Isaiah Berlin's *Karl Marx** (OUP) with an especially useful 'Guide to Further Reading' (by T. Carver). A biographical treat, which also contains biographies of Engels and Lenin, and of the idea of revolution and revolutionary socialism from Paris, via Marx's Rhineland and London, to Petrograd, is Edmund Wilson's *To the Finland Station* (Penguin).

Nick Jacobs 1994

About the author

Eduardo del Rio, better known as Rius, was born 1934 in Zamora, Michoacan, Mexico. From 1946 to 1951, he prepared for the priesthood in a Salesian seminary. In 1954, without formal art training, he converted to newspaper cartoonist. Prior to this, he had spells as a bottler, soap salesman, bookbinder, cashier and even gravedigger. Since 1954, Rius has been an unstoppable producer of political cartoons in nearly every Mexican newspaper and magazine, of two comic book series, *Underdogs* and *Supermachos*, directed four humour magazines, *The Chicken, Devil Mark, Gossip Illustrated* and *The Tick*, and fathered more than 70 books on every theme from medicine to Marx.

In 1968, his work won the Grand Prix de Montreal, and he has amassed international prizes from Bulgaria, Japan, Italy, Yugoslavia, Nicaragua, Brazil and other countries.

Rius is the only three-time winner of Mexico's National Magazine Prize. In 1969 he was arrested by the Mexican military and subjected to a mock execution for his part as a journalist gadfly in the '68 student movement. His books have been translated throughout the world.

Index